WESTERN TANTRA

THE WHITE PATH OF ETHICS

JAMES A. BEEBY

WESTERN TANTRA

Copyright © 2018 by James Addison Beeby, Jr.

Published by

Kaveinga Publishing

1259 El Camino Real, Suite 261

Menlo Park, CA 94025

kaveinga.publishing@outlook.com

ISBN: 978-1719147910

9 8 7 6 5 4 3 2 1

Cover and interior design by Domini Dragoone
Copy editor: Nona Strong
Cover photo: wjarek / Shutterstock.com
Printed in the United States of America

CONTENTS

PREFACE

This book is not for everyone; some people should not read it. If you take your religious scriptures literally as the product of a higher power unmodified by humans, Tantra definitely is not for you. The last thing I want to do is challenge your core beliefs. So if you think God himself reached down and wrote your scriptures in English or Hebrew or Arabic or Latin or whatever language as permanent instructions for all humans for all time, then I do not want to be the one to shake your faith. Step away from the book if you have not bought it, or close it and throw it in the trash if you have.

People who are completely happy with themselves and their traditional religion and have full confidence in its methods and results also have no reason to add Tantra. Most of the typical, established religions use faith and passive rescue as their primary methods for their followers. Have faith and you will be saved. Because passive rescue requires only faith and perhaps performing some inspiring rituals, it is safe. It requires no changes to the way you live your life or the way you view yourself. There must be many lovely people who can reach their ultimate potential in this life and the one beyond in this way. Tantra is not like this. Tantra requires change from you. Change involves risk. Tantra is not safe.

I wrote this for the people who are not in church on Sunday mornings. If you find the idea of a man on a throne in the heavens dispensing justice absurd or impossible, then Tantra may be for you. If you are an ethical atheist, or are devout but offended by what religions do to kill and persecute others in the name of their religion, then Tantra may be for you. If you would like to believe in a compassionate higher power but see no evidence that one exists, then Tantra may be for you. If you are open-minded and curious about Tantric practices but have no time to study ancient texts or attend lengthy lessons, then this version of Tantra may be for you. And if you are a religious leader who cannot fill the seats in your church, temple, synagogue, or mosque, but do not believe in the tenets put forth by the mega-churches, then Tantra may also be for you because Buddhism *does* fill its venues. Tantra can be used as a philosophy in combination with any religion and has never been limited to one religious path.

But if you are a fundamentalist in any religion and you are still reading this, please stop. Most of the people I have listed as readers are people you have already written off as hopeless. The people who now turn these pages rejected literal interpretations of scriptures long before I wrote this book and are no threat to your beliefs now—unless you keep reading. Tantra challenges traditional beliefs. My mother was a book illustrator who received death threats for portraying Mary and the baby Jesus as olive-skinned Middle Eastern Jews, as if this were some major threat to their core beliefs of Jesus as a white-skinned male with European features. I do not need this kind of aggravation, and you do not need the bad karma, so just stop reading. Put the book down now and go away. I mean it.

FOR THOSE OF YOU WHO are still here with me, the next question is—what are my qualifications for writing this? Here in the developed Western countries, the usual credential we expect is a doctorate degree. These are for the gods of our culture. I do not have one of those. Sorry. I made too many mistakes and wrong choices in life for that. I struggled for a B average in high school and managed to score in the 95th percentile on the college aptitude tests and the 99th percentile on the National Merit exam, but with my grades, that was only good enough for honorable mention. I was accepted into the tough Reed College physics program but essentially flunked out by the end of my first year. I transferred to Western Michigan University, where I tried other science courses and managed to graduate with a BS in psychology.

This was the peak of the Vietnam war, so my entire male graduating class was drafted. Not wanting to kill anyone, I thwarted the Army by enlisting in the United States Air Force as an officer. There my psychology degree netted me training in electronics (huh?) and four years stateside duty as a safety officer, advancing to the rank of Captain. While in the Air Force, I spent two years doing supervised volunteer work at Eastern State Hospital near Spokane, where psychology students occasionally mistook me for one of the inmates.

After the Air Force, my pregnant first ex-wife and I then moved so that I could spend two years in the Central Michigan University psychology master's program. There, in supervised clinical practice, I discovered that my problems were worse than those of my patients. We then moved to San Francisco, where I was unemployed until I landed my first safety position using my Air Force safety officer experience. Here I managed to complete a master's degree in safety from the University of Southern California in night school. I spent the next forty-plus years in the health and safety field, most of that working with scientists, successfully keeping them from killing themselves or setting their labs on fire— most of the time. In my spare time I designed and built a sailing catamaran, honing my engineering skills.

Two more children, my second divorce, and three unrequited loves later, a traumatic 1996 memory of a past life forced me to seek out a religion that accepted reincarnation. My cousin, a former monk, set me on the Tibetan Buddhist path, where for the last twenty years I have had both Buddhist and Christian mystical experiences that most people only read about. I worked with the homeless for about fifteen years. With thirty-five years of experience as an emergency responder, in 2003 I joined one of the federal search and rescue teams as a hazardous materials specialist, where I have been training ever since to respond to the next national disaster.

So those are my qualifications: fifty years as a smart adult making dumb mistakes; some forty years of raising children and protecting lives and the environment; thirty-five years of responding to medical injuries and industrial accidents; twenty years of intensive Tibetan Tantric practice and Christian mysticism; some fifteen years of difficult marriages and working with the homeless; ten years of college in physics, chemistry, biology, statistics, psychology, sociology, and safety to the master's level; four-and-a-half years of being a soldier in wartime without killing anyone; and three years of supervised work with the mentally ill, not counting myself. Much of this was concurrent, of course. Not a bad resume for life experience and performing altruistic acts in the real world, which is the essence of the book *Western Tantra, the White Path of*

Ethics as presented here. Now I hope you are not missing that doctorate degree, because I just do not see any time in my life where I could have squeezed that in.

IF DREAMS HAVE ANY VALIDITY, I may have a mandate to write the *Western Tantra* book. My first Tantric initiation was to Buddha Avalokiteshvara, the buddha of compassion, on 1 March 1998, by Geshe Lobsang Tsephel. The day before the initiation, Geshe Tsephel had given us instructions in how to stimulate dreaming on the eve of initiation, including prayers and sleeping on a strand of kusha grass. He said that what we dream on the eve of initiation may show our future on the Buddhist Path, if the signs preceding initiation are auspicious. My first dream that night was of flowing with a stream to the sea, which I later learned means the path to enlightenment in Buddhist symbolism.

Here is the second dream:

> *I am a poor immigrant on a modern ship bound for the New*
> *World. I am part of a large group of other poor immigrants*
> *who are crowded together in the cheapest accommodations*
> *on the ship, the steerage section in the stern mechanical area*
> *near the rudder. There is a large, high, open area in steerage,*
> *surrounded by walkways with railings filled with spectators.*
> *My fellow travelers and I are playing a game in the open*
> *area to pass our time on the long voyage. The game resembles*
> *baseball played on a diamond with a ball, pitcher, batters,*
> *and runners, but plays differently than American baseball. In*
> *this game, the pitcher hands off the ball to a player called the*
> *"snitch" (this was long before I ever heard of quidditch). The*
> *snitch runs the ball all around the diamond and all through*
> *the spectator area before finally delivering the ball to the*

*batter. After watching the game a while, I look out a porthole
and see the Statue of Liberty as we approach the New World.
Looking back at the game, I realize that this game on a
diamond will become the national pastime in the New World
after the game changes to allow the pitcher to pitch the ball
straight to the batter without the snitch as an intermediary,
and somehow I may play a part in this change.*

I awakened realizing the baseball game played on a diamond
symbolized Tantra, called the diamond path in Buddhism. The
pitcher was the teacher, and the ball represented the lesson for the
student, symbolized by the batter. The snitch represented the translator. When the translator is no longer required as an intermediary,
and the teacher can pitch the lesson straight to the student, then
Tantra will become the principal spiritual activity in the New World,
the developed West. Now that Tantra has come to the West, and
there are now many fine Western teachers who do not require translators, the time may be right for this dream to come true. Westerners
may be able to become enlightened entirely within the West.

THIS BOOK IS THE FIRST of three *Western Tantra* volumes. All three
lead to the same result, and each can stand alone or be used in
combination with the other two. This first volume is designed for
those who prefer doing ethical altruistic acts in the real world to
create positive karma, developing the capacity for universal, unconditional love. This is called *The White Path of Ethics*, white symbolizing skillful means and the crown energy center. The next volume
will be for those who have access to the spirit world of thought and
imagination, using meditation and prayer to renounce the material
world and develop mind control. This will be *The Red Path of Meditation*, red symbolizing wisdom and the throat and navel energy

centers. The third volume will be for those able to unify skillful means with wisdom to access the formless realm using stillness. This will be *The Blue Path of Union*, blue symbolizing union of skill and wisdom and the heart energy center.

Different Tantric systems use different colors, but these are just symbols, not inherently existing. You can use puce, magenta, and goldenrod for all I care. Together these three, the white, red and blue paths, make up the practices described in *Western Tantra*, working in the material, spirit, and formless realms which together make up totality. All three paths lead to the same outcome, becoming one with our divine nature, using different methods that can be used separately or in any combination with the other paths.

SOME OF YOU MAY NOT like my writing style. I tend to use simple words and repetition, which causes some readers to think that I "talk down to them" as if they lack intelligence. Not so. Spiritual concepts are difficult to grasp and I have the utmost respect for anyone who makes the attempt to understand. I write the way I do because I come to this from the health and safety field where clear instructions are a matter of life and death. I am not trying to sound scholarly, I am trying to be understood. For example, if you are navigating while your spouse is driving, you do not try to impress by saying things like, "Rotate sinistrally immediately!" Instead you go for clarity by saying, "Turn left now!" and maybe add, "Left at this corner" just to be clear. Similarly, the US Navy uses right and left for helm commands, not starboard and port. Repetition using slightly different phrasing is also important in critical situations. Once when I was in the Air Force a woman told me repeatedly, "Go up, go up, go up!" Unfortunately, I was driving a car at the time and going up was not an option. If she had tried different phrasing like, "turn north" or had pointed in the correct direction we would not have missed the turn. Like guiding a vehicle, traveling a spiritual path can also have life and death implications, how to live your life and how to die, and I may not be available to clarify certain points, so please forgive me if I go for simplicity and repetition. I do not think you are less intelligent than I am. I think you are too valuable to mislead. Also, I may swear occasionally to wake you up or emphasize a point. No disrespect is intended. Tantra is for mature adults.

MOST LIKELY, THE BOOK *WESTERN TANTRA* will evolve and change as those who practice it learn new information, and as time and conditions change the world and humanity. It will be wonderful if this book is error-free, but that is very unlikely. I have done the best I can with what I have to work with, but I am not perfect, so there have to be mistakes, probably in the underlying concepts. However I have tried everything written here, and it all worked for me, so most of this is at least functionally correct, even if some of the details are wrong. Please do not throw out the whole book if I have made a few errors. If something seems wrong, my Buddhist teachers instructed me to put these things in a compartment in the mind labeled "maybe wrong and needs verification" rather than just rejecting the ideas outright. Also do not hold onto ideas just because they confirm what you already believe or want to believe. You should also be ready to let go or modify even cherished concepts if you find they are not true, based on reliable new information. If reliable new information contradicts anything I have written here, I will certainly revise the content to reflect the new information. So if something works or does not work for you, feel free to contact me through the publisher to let me know. With that request and promise, welcome to my book.

—James A. Beeby
April 2018

ACKNOWLEDGEMENTS

This book would not have been possible without the following people. My mother and father gave birth to my current body and raised it to adulthood. My mother taught me creativity and my father taught me steadfastness. My extended family, which includes teachers and authors, taught me the value of education and expression. My children taught me unconditional love and parenting skills. My Uncle Sam gave me freedom, my safety career, and the retirement income that allows me time to write. My search-and-rescue team members let me see angels at work. I cannot think of any relative or friend who has not contributed something to this work.

My cousin and former monk, Steve Pearl, started me on the Buddhist path at a time of desperate need. My first Buddhist lecture by Robert Thurmond on death and dying confirmed I was on the right path. Lama Thubten Yeshe and Lama Zopa Rinpoche founded the FPMT, the Foundation for the Preservation of Mahayana Tradition, which supplied a uniformly excellent staff of teachers and courses to me and the other Western students. Sadly the list of teachers I am indebted to is too long to recite, and I would risk forgetting some if I tried to name them all. But you teachers know who you are.

Other Buddhist teachers who were not part of the FPMT included His Holiness the Dalai Lama, Geshe Michael Roach, and Thich Nhat Hanh.

My Christian guides and teachers included Father Calvin Rutherford, Bishop William Swing, Father Thomas Hand, and Father Thomas Keating.

I am grateful to the following California spiritual centers that are my "pure lands" and at a difficult time in my life were the only places on Earth where I felt accepted and welcome. These are the Vajrapani Institute in Boulder Creek and the Tse Chen Ling dharma center in San Francisco, Transfiguration Episcopal Church in San Mateo, Grace Cathedral in San Francisco, Mercy Center in Burlingame, and more recently Saint Pius Catholic Church in Redwood City, along with the staffs at each of these centers.

I thank the people in my spiritual support groups, my "soul friends," who let me express my ideas and smooth my rough edges. These include all the members of the Saint Pius Interfaith Dialog Group, plus Kelly Joyce Neff, Matt Reeve, and Gyalten Yangchen. In fact, everyone I have ever met has contributed in one way or another. Thank you all.

CHAPTER 1

THE WHITE PATH OF ETHICAL ACTION

"Work is love made visible."

—KAHLIL GHIBRAN

To some of us, the world looks seriously fucked up. Something in our lives is broken, and we have no idea what that is, much less how to fix it. Things that used to work no longer do. Activities that used to bring joy now seem more like chores. We are as the dead walking, the gum chewed too long that has lost its flavor. Problems come so fast we have new problems before we have solved the old ones. Objectively, everything is okay; we have what we need, but life feels as if something really important is missing. What's going on? What's happening to us? Rejoice, for when your life feels like this, you are approaching the gateway to a better life.

We might be immortal beings. Countless wise men and women have said so, and equally wise people have said no. We will start with the premise that we are immortal. Why? Well, if the one-life-and-when-we-are-dead-we-no-longer-exist folks are correct, then when you die there is nothing to do and nothing to worry about; you no longer exist. But if you live your life with this view and you are wrong, then you are completely unprepared for what happens next. So the safe position is to assume that our consciousness endures beyond this life, to investigate if this could be true, what form it could take, and how one should prepare for it. We will investigate this in these chapters. More importantly, we will give you the tools to find your own answers.

A lot of people just accept what their parents or friends or advisors say is true. If you do this you are putting your future in the hands of others. Frankly, a lot of what people believe is just nuts. Some believe there is a list of rules that we have to follow, and some guy sitting in the stars somewhere will judge how well we followed the rules and assign us to a lovely place or a place of eternal torment, depending on how well we do. Really? Some believe that they can buy their way into the good place, or they can do horrible things to others for their entire lives and get to go to the good place as long as they confess their sins on their deathbed. Really? Many believe that people who have helped others for their entire lives but did not submit to the guy in the stars, or maybe never even heard about him, are doomed. Really? These beliefs are really fucked up. And some people wonder why others reject their beliefs and choose other beliefs or why some people are atheists.

Here is the way things are. All of the world's major religions and philosophies once had a person or a few inspired founders who grasped an aspect of reality resulting in achieving harmony with reality and improving the lives of others at a particular place and moment of time. Typically the larger society resisted the new society formed by the enlightened founders, because their new ideas conflicted with the established ideas that formed the larger soci-ety's life plans for people. Old society then tried to destroy the new society, and the new society had to harden its belief system to avoid destruction. New society codified its dogma, even carving it into stone. Eventually, if the new belief system performed better than the old one at that time and place, then the new replaced the old.

But to resist the old, the new beliefs had already been codified and became rigid. Worse, as time passed, the inspired founders and those who knew them were no longer around to interpret their words and explain their practices. Consequently, some of the more puzzling statements like "love your enemies" or "surrender" or "all things are empty" became translated into languages that did not have the correct words or were interpreted by people who were not as inspired or enlightened as the founders of that belief system. Thus the religion or philosophy degenerated.

In Buddhism it is said that an enlightened being cuts through illusion and creates a new belief system in harmony with reality, and thereafter the belief system degenerates until it no longer resembles the original. Religions make a copy of a copy until the original can no longer be understood. If you think about it, this cannot be any other way. This is the way it must be.

So what is the value of established religions and philosophies, if any? The value is that they preserve the ancient writings of the enlightened founders, writings which contain universal truths that may still apply to this time and place. How do we apply these truths when we do not know what the inspired founders actually said or meant? We do this by looking for the meaning beneath the words, the energy driving the action. Ask what deep unspoken or unspeakable belief or attitude would cause the inspired founder to say or do what was said or done in that particular situation in that time and place. For example, Jesus once said to a group about to stone an adulteress, "Let him who is without sin among you be the first to cast a stone at her (John 8:7, St. Joseph edition)." Stoning was the punishment prescribed by Jewish law at that time. The new rule Jesus introduced was to forgive, because no one is perfect. This new rule conflicted with the established rule, and this put Jesus himself in danger. Why would he risk the consequences of defying established law? Looking deeply beneath the words describing this event, unconditional love for others comes to mind.

Would Jesus's life plan work in this time and place? Suppose you are married with children and you learn your spouse has had sex with another. You could kill your spouse or the lover and go to prison. You could leave and divide resources and your time with the children. You could hold a grudge against your spouse, living the rest of your lives together in tension and anger. You could discuss the issues, forgive, and try to do better in the future. Many have chosen each of these options. Which choice would have the better outcome?

If you read ancient writings and decide to try to love all people unconditionally and forgive those who hurt you, and this works for you, then the ancient writings have helped you, whether or not the words are true or fiction, mere myths designed to teach something. That is the value of established religions and philosophies, to preserve the ancient writings for possible use in our time. Even the works of early scientists were preserved in monasteries during the Dark Ages and the Middle Ages, both times of inquisition and destruction of knowledge.

The bits of wisdom contained in ancient writings are, after all, just signs marking a trail of someone who has gone that way before. If others have followed that way and reported benefits, then what does it matter who wrote or if the writings meet a bulletproof concept of reality? For example, if you knock on a door, it is not important that you know that the door is almost entirely empty space and that your knuckles do not touch the door but rather interact with the electromagnetic forces between the subatomic particles of your knuckles and the subatomic particles of the door. It is enough that you know to rap your knuckles on a device labeled a door to create a sound to alert someone inside to unlock it and let you pass through the doorway to encounter what is on the other side. The functional concept of knocking on the door is enough to see you through.

If however, you need to walk through the closed and locked door as described in the writings of some religious traditions, then you need a deep understanding of the physics underlying apparent reality. Mostly this book will work with functional reality, and we will not worry too much about precision. If a technique works, use it and do not worry if the underlying concept is completely accurate. Occasionally we may speculate about the nature of true reality and see if it lets us pass through some locked doors that seem to deny entry to other people.

THE ESSENCE OF THIS BOOK is Tantra, which in Sanskrit means "to weave," as in to interweave your thread of life with that of others to create a tapestry, an integrated whole that serves a purpose or tells a story. The essence of Tantra is to use everything you have to transform yourself from an unhappy limited mortal to one who is in contact with what we call the eternal and infinite. Tantric practices date back to the Hindu religion and probably have roots further back in time than that. This is ancient Tantra, not the modern neotantra that has no relationship to true Tantra. True Tantric techniques can be used to supplement any religious or non-religious practices. Tantra is famous, possibly infamous, for its sexual practices, and we will cover those in this book. But Tantra extends beyond the sexual arena and can encompass all aspects of life.

I learned Tantra from Tibetan Buddhist teachers and still practice Tantra in that form, but I came to realize that a lot of what I was taught was Tibetan culture and tradition. These are profound and very beautiful but are not essential to Tantric practices, which are universal and can be used with any compassionate religion or philosophy. The universal aspect of Tantra is to see ourselves and to act at all times as if we have actually achieved the ultimate goal any person can reach, our highest potential, our deepest wish. So if you are Buddhist wishing to become a buddha, you act at all times as if you are already an enlightened buddha with a heart of loving compassion for all. If you are Christian wishing to become an angel or saint, then you act at all times as Christ would have acted. The same goes for any religion or belief system, including atheism. In all cases you will hopefully be helping all others in any way possible without regard to race, religion, social status, or any other culturally assigned labels to the best of your knowledge and the extent of your resources. Be what you want to become.

The techniques of Tantra harness the power of your emotions to drive your vision of your transformation. Pleasure, pain, anger, jealousy, sex, love, whatever you have—transmute these and use their energy as the power to change yourself. Used carelessly and selfishly, sexuality and other emotions can be very destructive to yourself and others, so Tantra is known as a potentially dangerous path with many pitfalls. But emotions are also honest and have great power that can accelerate transformation when used with skill and care. Because of this, Tantra is known as the lightning path to transformation, the fast path. With our desire for fast results and our impatience for delay, Tantra is ideal for Westerners with our over-amped lifestyles.

The term Western Tantra as a specific practice is the universal aspect of the traditional forms of Tantra practiced in the Eastern religions, stripped of its Eastern cultural trappings and reframed and repopulated with the cultural foundations of the Western nations. This term does not refer to neotantra or its modern practices. As far as I know, this book is the first to use the term Western Tantra to refer to reframing traditional Eastern Tantra for use in the West. Why reframe Tantra? Eastern Tantra is tailored to the Eastern nations which have different histories, mindsets, and traditions that seem very foreign and unrealistic to Westerners. Stories of flying statues, magic jewels and such make us question other concepts which may be true. In the West we are also suspicious of placing blind faith in any spiritual leader as followers of the Eastern religions may do. And Eastern people have less problem with lengthy teachings which may take hours or days to convey an essential point.

Here in the West, we value science and have nearly elevated it to a religion. If someone says that something is definitely true, we want them to provide proof and get straight to the point without wasting our time. So in this book I take the position that truth does not conflict with truth, and scientific theories that have been well proven, such as evolution and the age of the universe, are probably true. Any belief system that aims to penetrate the heart of reality should not contradict well established scientific truths.

Of course, what we perceive as factual depends on our points of view and our definitions of terms. For example, I define God as the entire universe or multiverse, all that exists or ever could exist, both seen and unseen. So by my definition, we are all in God and God is in us, just as the mystics say. Defined as the entire universe, all but extreme nihilists believe in God, including you atheists out there. The only debates remaining are whether the universe is conscious and whether it cares about us.

The general method that characterizes the Path of Ethics is ethical action in the material world. Action means doing something tangible and visible. Ethical action is action which is intended to benefit others, or at least benefit most people with the least harm to the fewest number. Intent is important because we are creatures of limited perception, so sometimes our intended results do not turn out the way we expect. Just be sure that our intent to benefit is what we planned up front and not something we invent after the shit hits the fan. The ordinary material world is where we do our work for the Path of Ethics. The powers of prayer, meditation and more esoteric practices belong to other paths, as explained in the Preface. There are many paths for different types of people and all lead to the same place. On the Path of Ethics we work in the ordinary world, feeding the hungry, comforting the sick, giving pleasure, and transforming ourselves and others through our actions. Labeling the Path of Ethics the White Path is Buddhist symbolism. White symbolizes skillful means, how to accomplish things. This the "get-it-done" path to personal transformation.

HOMEWORK:

At the end of each chapter I will suggest work to do "after class," so to speak. Reading this does no good if you don't do anything differently. Nothing will happen if you don't apply the lessons to your life. For this first chapter, try this. Whenever you are outside, at work, or at home, keep your cell phone in its place and instead look around you. If you see someone in distress, ask what is wrong and comfort them. If you see a homeless person, acknowledge their presence. If someone asks for money, give some or a food coupon or at least a word of regret. If someone helps you, thank them. If someone compliments your work, give credit to any who helped you. In other words, be present in the world and react kindly and unselfishly to whatever happens around you.

Try this for at least a month and see what happens. Write down any significant events. If this is not your normal mode of being, be prepared to give people who know you an explanation for your changed behavior, and assure them that you are okay and not in need of therapy.

FURTHER READING:

The book *Western Tantra* is intended to stand alone, needing only application by its readers to test the concepts in their own lives to see if they work. However, in the interest of getting straight to the point without excessive detail, these instructions may be too sparse even for Westerners. If this is the case, or you would like to explore a topic in more depth, suggestions for further reading will be provided.

Here is a suggestion for reading about the universal aspects of religion and philosophy. *The Perennial Philosophy* by Aldous Huxley describes the universal themes and beliefs that are found in all religions and philosophies.

CHAPTER 2

TANTRIC TERMS

"When I use a word," Humpty Dumpty said,
in a rather scornful tone, "it means just what
I choose it to mean—neither more nor less."

"The question is," said Alice, "whether you CAN
make words mean so many different things."

"The question is," said Humpty Dumpty,
"which is to be master—that's all."

—LEWIS CARROLL, *THROUGH THE LOOKING GLASS*

W ords have many different meanings. In order to understand what I write here, you need to understand how I define the terms I use. When a word is in lower case, I am just using the word as ordinarily understood in context and defined in *Webster's Dictionary*, specifically *Webster's Seventh New Collegiate Dictionary*. I know, it is old and an actual book and technically an antique, but that is the one I have and use. For modern terms not in this dictionary I look for consensus on the Internet.

Except for proper names, when I capitalize a term, it means I have given it a specific definition somewhere in this book, either the first time it is used, or in this chapter, or in the Glossary. For many, religious terms are emotionally charged and have many different meanings for different people. It is very important that you understand the way I am defining these terms. I may upset some people with the way I view some religious or philosophical concepts, but please, only be upset with the way that I really mean to use the words, not the way you may use the same words. Religious wars have started over misunderstandings in languages and terms, when there may have been little or no actual disagreement had they understood the differences in the way the opposing sides used different words. In the previous chapter I defined how we will be using the terms Tantra, Western Tantra, God, Path of Ethics, and White Path.

We will be using several other key terms. Western Tantra uses many of these terms differently than other spiritual, religious, philosophical, medical, and scientific frameworks. A primary source of misunderstanding among people is the use of the same words differently or different words to describe the same thing. For example, a fundamentalist Christian might say that God is a being on a throne in heaven who made the world a few thousand years ago, and a Buddhist and a scientist might then say that God does not exist. Then a mystical Christian may say the other Christian is wrong, God is the ineffable which pervades all things manifest and all things come into existence from God and eventually return to God. The Buddhist then says she believes in that, but they call that Emptiness. The fundamentalist says that is blasphemy. The scientist says there is no way to test that, so there is no way to prove it is true. The mystical Christian then says Emptiness is a terrible way to describe God and says Fullness is a better word. The scientist says he does not believe in anything he cannot prove. The fundamentalist then says all of you but me are going to eternal hell. The Buddhist tells the fundamentalist that hell is a mere state of mind, and he is in hell already, but there is a way out of hell. The scientist then says the rest of you are nuts for believing things that do not exist. This argument can go on forever unless the parties agree on what they mean by the terms they use.

With any use of words to represent ideas, it is impossible for the reader to understand what the writer means without the writer first explaining how the terms will be used. After defining terms, we still may not agree, but at least you will understand what I am trying to convey. These terms are compiled from a broad range of religious and scientific texts. None of them are new terms or unique uses, but most have different meanings, so the meaning I will be using will be explained here. Again, whenever a term is used in a particular way, it will be capitalized, and the meaning for the term will be listed here or the first time it is used in the text or in the Glossary. Capitalized words that are italicized are book titles. Lower case terms are defined by context and common usage as listed in *Webster's*. I will group Western Tantric terms into the general areas discussed next.

✄ **REALMS OF EXISTENCE:** Western Tantra divides existence into three primary realms or aspects, defined here as Material, Spirit, and Divine. Together they make up a triune Reality.

Material: The realm we ordinarily experience is the Material or Physical realm or world, the physical universe made up of ordinary matter and energy that we can experience with our body senses, and that science can measure with instruments. This is one of the two Form realms. Note that ordinary energy is included in this category. All three realms of existence are "real" in the sense that they exist; however when Real is capitalized here, it will refer to the Material realm, the one that everyone agrees exists. The Path of Ethics operates mainly in the Real world. Synonyms: Physical, Real, Visible

Spirit: The other Form realm, related to the Material realm, is the Spirit or Mental Form realm or world, the world of words, ideas, concepts, thoughts, images, projections, states of mind, dreams and visions including visualized forms. As products of consciousness, with effort and the right conditions we can turn most images, ideas, concepts, dreams and visions into Real things. Conversely, we can say ideas that cannot be made Real are fantasy, yet they are still manifested as images and belong to this world of dreams and visions. The Spirit realm has the richest diversity. Pure lands, heavens, and hells are here. Religions that assign their supreme beings definite form and characteristics place them in this realm by definition. The concepts of Ego and Self live here. Thought rules here. Synonyms: Thought, Imaginary, Fantasy, Word, Concept, Ghost, Dream, Between, Beyond, Bardo, Mental Form

Divine: Both the Material Form realm and the Spirit Form realm are thought to arise from a third realm, the Divine or Formless, which pervades all realms of existence. Buddhists call this Emptiness, meaning empty of fixed inherent existence. Many are not aware of the Formless. The Formless is Pure Potential, anything that could exist. Consciousness acting on the Formless brings Form into existence. Wave functions may be part of this realm, and quantum mechanics may be touching on this aspect of reality. The unwritten laws of the universe, which determine all reality, are placed here. The Observer, our Soul, lives here as do Love, joy and awe. God-concepts described as nameless, secret, and unknowable belong here. Consciousness rules here. Synonyms: Formless,

Eternal, Ultimate, Un-manifest, Ineffable, Transcendent, Beyond the Beyond, Unknowing, Emptiness, Fullness, Infinity, Ground State, Pure Potential, Pure Awareness

✖ HUMAN ELEMENTS: Western Tantra divides humans into three elements or aspects that correspond to the three realms of existence and together make up a human being. We are made of Body, Ego, and Soul.

Body: We have a physical human Body in the Material realm made up of matter and energy. The Body has a mostly fixed form and is mortal, having a finite lifespan. The Body has a thinking organ called the brain which we will call the Head or Body-Mind. Body sensory organs gather information from the outside world in the form of nerve impulses that are sent to the Head where they can be processed or stored as needed. Discursive thought and reasoning take place in the Head, the physical brain. The brain is capable of thought using physical and chemical processes to create brain patterns representing mental constructs called words, numbers, symbols, and images. These brain patterns represent aspects of outer reality derived from stored sensory information that we call memory. Every time memory is recalled, it can be changed before it is stored again. New sensory information is compared to past memory information, and the Head works out predictions of future outcomes to determine actions needed in the present. This process takes time. Even well practiced thoughts and actions take a few tenths of a second, so the Body and Head exist in the Present, but their perceptions, thoughts and actions always lag slightly behind current reality.

Ego: As we accumulate memories of experiences, we develop images of ourselves that more or less correspond to the way we look physically, the way others tell us we look and act, and the ways we typically relate to the world. This set of Form images exists in the realm of thought, the Spirit realm. Because this self-image is created by thought, we call it our False Self or Ego. Other terms for our self-image or images of others are Personality, Spirit, Apparition, and Ghost, and we will use these terms as synonyms for Ego. Because our Body has a fixed form, most people think Personality also cannot be changed, but because self-image is created by thought, we can change if we free ourselves from habitual thought patterns. I am not sure our Ego has thinking functions, but assuming it has, we will refer to this as Ego Mind or Selfish Mind, our habitual ways of thinking. I suspect Ego Mind is a mental construct with a point of view or focus of attention which can be anywhere in time and space. If Ego Mind does not have its own thinking functions, it may just focus its attention on the Body's brain for rational thought or the Soul's Heart for intuition. Ego Mind can be changed and trained to be still. The spiritual journey is often described as moving our point of view from the Head to the Heart. Because the Spirit is a mental concept with no Physical reality, it does not necessarily die with the body. If adopted and fed by the immortal Soul, Spirit can be carried to the next life. Synonyms for our human Spirit realm aspect as used here include Ego, False Self, Personality, Spirit, Apparition, and Ghost.

Soul: Here we use the term Soul to designate our deepest ultimate nature or aspect, pure consciousness dwelling in the Formless realm, our Divine nature, our pearl of great price, the pure light hidden within each of us, our ground state of being, the godhead within. Soul is formless and without boundaries. Like the Formless realm, many are not aware of the Soul. Soul may be immortal. In a human life our Soul seems to be centered in the Body near the physical heart but may extend beyond the Body. We will call the sentient aspect of the Soul the Heart, Heart-Mind, Intuitive Mind, the seat of consciousness, or Subtle Mind. Heart thoughts are called no-thought, intuition, doing without thinking, or instant knowing. Instant knowing is like a burst transmission, containing compressed meaning that can be instantly available or can be unpacked to play out over time in the realm of thought as emotions, poetry, art, music and dreams. Soul senses are direct contact with reality; this may be the "third eye." Soul is the source of creativity and our sense of the eternal. With it prophets can see past, present, and future. Soul can catch up to the present moment with no lag and can process events in "Bullet-Time." Synonyms used here for Soul are True Self, True Nature, No-Self, Godhead, The Observer, The Witness, Subtle Consciousness or Subtle Mind.

✂ TIME ELEMENTS: Time is a dimension of the Universe that is used to express the duration of existence and the rate of change. Time has three elements Buddhists call "The Three Times," Past, Present, and Future.

Past: The past is something that already happened and cannot be changed. What we call the Past is related to our particular location, velocity and acceleration; the Past is relative to where we are. For example, a star may have exploded billions of years ago, but if the light has just reached us we may say it is happening now. But conceptually, we know we are seeing ancient history, and there is no way we can affect the supernova, so we realize that event is actually in our Past. The Past is what we use to predict the Future. Synonyms: History, Then, Back

Present: This is the currently active moment of time, based on our particular location in space-time. This is the only moment when reality is fluid and we can change what is happening. Free

Will is our ability to affect the Present. From our perspective only the Present moment exists, and Time is an arrow that points and moves only to the Future, although physics says time is flexible and may be reversible. Synonyms: Now, In-the-Moment

Future: This aspect of time is what is affected by what happens in the Present. At any given moment of time, the Future exists only as a set of probabilities for what may happen. By our actions in the Present, we can affect which Future probabilities become the next Present moment. Synonym: Next.

✂ KARMA: This is the relationship between effects and their causes. For we who live in Linear Time, a cause is something which precedes and determines an effect. So in the Present moment, we are experiencing effects determined by causes that occurred in the Past, and our actions in the Present are causes that become effects in the Future. Karma can also refer to the effects that have occurred or will occur as a result of our prior thoughts, words, or deeds. Karma is often described as positive or negative, based on whether our actions were intended to benefit or harm others. Causes in this life carry over into the next life if they were not experienced in this one. Synonym: Cause and Effect

Linear Time: Time which progresses from Past to Present to Future with no branches. This is the time we ordinary human beings perceive, but this may not be universal.

Bullet-Time: As seen in the movie *The Matrix*, Bullet-Time is experiencing reality with the faster speed of the Soul rather than the normal speed of the human brain. In Bullet-Time events seem to slow down, giving us plenty of time to react to whatever is happening. Many people have experienced this. Figuratively speaking, we have time to see and dodge bullets. Please don't try this at home.

✂ **RELIABILITY TERMS**: Here are definitions and synonyms for some terms relating to whether or not we can rely on information and concepts.

False: Frequently used in Eastern Tantric texts, whether capitalized or not, false designates something that appears to be true but is not. The important thing to note is that false things only appear to be true, as opposed to things that are obviously wrong. Synonym: Illusory

True: Often used incorrectly in Eastern Tantric texts, here in accordance with *Webster's*, True and Truth designate something that is correct, real, and can be relied on.

Fact: A Fact is something generally accepted as accurate from a particular point of view, relative to the user. The opposites of Fact are Fiction and Lies. For example, asserting something is "fast" is different for turtles, rabbits, jet pilots, and linear accelerator operators. Each of us lives in a different world, a different reality. Democrat Facts are Republican Fiction and Lies and vice versa. This differs from the conventional definition which assumes facts are independently and inherently accurate for everyone. It is a mistake to try to impose your Facts on another person living a different reality from yours.

✂ **OTHER TERMS**: Here are some other definitions and synonyms which reflect the way we will be using the terms listed.

Enlightened: Western Tantra does not use the ordinary sense of this term to refer to people who are really smart and think in modern analytical ways, using reason rather than magic and superstition. As used here, capitalized, Enlightened or Enlightenment refers to the Buddhist use of the term meaning a consciousness that has full access to the formless Divine realm, as well as complete

access to the Material and Spirit form realms. The Christian translation of this term is one who is in union with God.

Form: Form means having some sort of manifestation. This
manifestation can be either physical or mental. Physical Forms
include visible and touchable things, sounds, smells, and energy
that can be sensed with the ordinary body senses and with scientific instruments. These are things made of ordinary matter
or energy that make up the Material world. Mental Forms are
thoughts and concepts that can be imagined in the mind, including mental representations of words, numbers, symbols, sounds,
smells, ideas, images, visions, concepts, and anything else that can
be represented in our minds. These are made of thought, not matter or ordinary energy, but they can be sensed in the "mind's eye."
There are two Form realms of existence: The Material world, made
of physical Forms, and the Spirit world, made of Mental Forms. A
synonym for Form is Manifest.

God: As used in this book, God is defined as the entire
universe or multiverse encompassing everything: all that ever
existed, exists now, or ever could exist, both seen and unseen,
Form and Formless. We hope to establish that this universe is
conscious and cares about us. Tantra views Divine consciousness
as male and female aspects united, both rather than neither, so
there is no pronoun like he, she, or it that accurately applies. In
the book *Western Tantra* we will try to avoid the use of pronouns
when referring to God or Ultimate Reality. Where the use of
pronouns is unavoidable, understand that we mean all aspects
of Totality which includes everything, not just male or female.
Synonyms for God used here include Universe, Ultimate, Reality, Totality, All, Infinity, Emptiness, Fullness, Allah, and Yahweh, but there are many other terms for God used by the world's
religions and philosophies.

I: The focus of each person's attention or concentration is our "I, me, or my" point of view. Its location is usually in the Head, attending to the sensory information from the Body and to one's thoughts. Our focus of attention is very mobile and can be almost anywhere. The spiritual journey is often called moving our focus of attention from our Head to our Heart or from the Ego to the Soul. When our focus of attention is our Heart, the seat of consciousness, we have access to intuition. The "I" is who we say we are, as in "I am" this or that. Most people use "I" to designate their Ego, but those who identify with Soul and have become selfless still have to use the words "I, me, and my" to refer to themselves when inhabiting a human body.

Love: The word love has many meanings including sex, craving, attraction, affection, attachment, devotion, even zero. When capitalized in this book, Love means universal unconditional love or the energy and power of unconditional love for all. Literally, love with no conditions whatsoever. This is the Love often seen between parents and their children, between some pets and their owners (not sure about cats), and without exception between God and humanity. What naturally follows from Love is the wish to provide all living beings with pleasure and to remove pain from all beings who are suffering, which we call compassion. Love is the principal practice of Western Tantra.

Mystic, Mystical: The Mystic is one who has a direct link to the Divine realm or to the Spirit world acting as an intermediary to the Divine realm. The Mystic gets instructions and knowledge directly from Ultimate Reality rather than from scriptures. Mystical means that which is in direct contact with Ultimate Reality. Because Mystics speak and act according to an open Heart of Love in contact with God, Mystics often violate dogma and rigid laws, putting them in conflict with institutional religions. Mystics are often persecuted and executed. As used here, Mystic and Mystical do not refer to neotantric, occult, or "dark magic" practices in any way, although institutional religions distrust Mystics and often try to discredit them by branding them with these labels.

Occam's razor: This is a philosophical and scientific principle stating that among competing theories, the one with the fewest assumptions should be selected as the one most likely to be true.

Path: A series of steps used to get you from where you are to where you want to be is called a path or journey. The term is broad and is often not used literally as a physical track on the ground to get to a place. Less literally, Polynesians navigated between islands by means of a star path called kaveinga. Even more figuratively, we refer to a recipe or formula for success as the path to greatness. Used in its capitalized form here, the term Path refers to a set of techniques to reach Ultimate Reality. Some spiritual writers insist there is no spiritual path, but they are taking the term literally. Spiritual paths are *always* meant figuratively as a recipe or steps to achieve spiritual realizations. Synonyms for Path include Way, Journey, Road, Vehicle.

Tool: A Tool refers to a single technique or method that will help achieve a particular objective as part of the Western Tantric Path.

HOMEWORK:

1. Try this. Hold a book of fiction and read it out loud while walking around your home or some safe location. Don't stop reading or walking. While reading, visualize what is happening in the book. Also note your changing mood as you read. What do you think others will think if they see you doing this? Without stopping any of these activities, start wondering how long you

should waste your time doing this when you have so many other things to do, and decide what to do next. Set a time to stop, and occasionally check the time. When you reach your allotted time, sit down, grab pencil and paper, and list all the things you were able to do at the same time. Include breathing, pumping blood, digesting food, seeing and reading, seeing and navigating, sensing time, visualizing, and emoting. Also list all the thoughts you had concurrently. Then after each item on the list, write down which mind you think was overseeing that activity and where you think it was located. How many independent thought and sense processors did you come up with? Do you think it all happened in the brain, or can some of the activities be assigned to the Ego or Soul mind? Do you think you are a single entity or a well-coordinated collection?

2. Also try this. Without giving any hints, ask a number of people to point to themselves. Note how many pointed to their head. Probably not many. Do you think those who pointed to the center of their chest were aware of their actual center of being?

FURTHER READING:

John O'Donohue in *Anam Cara* has a lyrical way of describing the Celtic spirituality that can apply to all spiritual paths. His description of the Celtic soul is compatible with the Western Tantric view of Soul.

CHAPTER 3

WESTERN CULTURE

"The mind may never rest in the sure knowledge of the
truth unless it finds it by the method of experiment."

—ROGER BACON, *OPUS MAJUS*

What do we mean by "Western" as opposed to Eastern, and what characterizes it? The West is the collection of democratic, pluralistic countries of the developed West; occidental; a nebulous area of the world that everyone understands but no one can clearly define. Roughly this means regions influenced by European cultures. Cultural belief systems of the Western world include democracy, individual and personal freedom, equality, human rights, the Abrahamic religions, capitalism, science and the scientific method, and public education. Although changing as the world becomes smaller and more similar, Western countries as a group are strong economically because of an emphasis on science and engineering, applying these to achieve results.

Westerners tend not to trust in magic to solve problems, and at least for now, want proof before believing something is true. For that reason, it is harder for Western people to accept Eastern religious and spiritual practices, because the underlying philosophy of why they work is not compatible with Western culture. This book is an attempt to reframe the practice of Tantra in terms Westerners can understand.

One of the fundamental belief systems of Western culture is the scientific method, a systematic approach to determining the laws defining reality, what is real and why, and how this knowledge can be applied to do things thought to be impossible. For example, by applying the laws of chemistry and physics, humans reached the moon. Personally, I do not see any incompatibility between science and religion. I like to think that God as the conscious and sentient universe is just as interested in the science of how the universe works as we are in the science of how our bodies work. It is possible that scientists are God's mirrors and microscopes, doing God's work and protecting God's worlds.

A fundamental principal of Western Tantra is this: truth cannot conflict with truth. If evidence shows something may be true, then it is worth exploring to find out if it is true, even if it conflicts with long-held beliefs. If something can be shown to be true or reliably functions as a result of some underlying truth, then it must be accepted, and conflicting concepts must be adjusted to account for the new reality. For example, people used to believe the world is flat, therefore it must have edges, and if one were to pass beyond the edge, they would fall to their doom. This discouraged exploration out of fear of what lay beyond the familiar. Eventually scientists found evidence that the world is a sphere, therefore one must be able to reach the east by travelling west. Explorers relying on the evidence generated by scientists were able to prove that to be true by actually sailing west. The world then adjusted its concepts to account for both truths: the world looks flat locally because it is really big, and you cannot see the curve over short distances, but globally it makes a difference for long-distance travel. Yet flat pool tables still function just fine over short distances.

Note that while it is the scientists who gather evidence and develop theories of reality, it is often others who prove them true. I will call these others "explorers," those with the courage and means to test the theories. We will try to do both parts here, develop theories of what lies Beyond and how to get there based on evidence, then have the courage to explore to see if the theories are true.

✺ THE SCIENTIFIC METHOD: Here is a short outline of the scientific method. It is simplified but will work well enough for our purposes. First we define a problem we want to solve or a question we want answered. Then we collect existing information relating to the problem or question, trying to be comprehensive and unbiased, open to all possible solutions and answers. Note that if we collect only information supporting our prior beliefs and preferences, then we have most likely predetermined the results of our inquiry, and we might as well have not bothered to do the research. So we must be open-minded and have the courage to challenge existing beliefs. Also note that we must not be biased about where and when we collect data, or any conclusions we reach may only apply to the population, location, and time where we collected information. For example, many toxicity studies apply only to lab rats, and many psychological studies apply only to college students. So we must step out of our comfort zone when collecting initial information.

Once we have collected existing information about the question or problem we want to solve, including our own observations, we need to list all the possible answers or solutions that would account for existing data. We then develop theories to explain the data.

Next we examine the existing data supporting or refuting each theory to see how reliable we consider the sources. Based on evidence, logic, and yes even personal bias, the scientist selects a theory to test. Most scientists know they cannot know or prove the entire body of human knowledge on their own, but they may be able to add important ideas about what-is and how things work. It is perfectly acceptable to choose what areas of human knowledge we choose to explore.

Once we have picked a theory to test, the next step is to figure out a way to test it to determine if it is true or not. Sometimes this is done by process of elimination, proving all other possibilities false or unsuccessful. Other ways include making predictions of outcomes of experiments based on the theory we are testing. If different conditions, called variables, could affect the result, we must either control them or account for the variability statistically. In any event, we must develop a plan for testing our theory, actually do the testing, and collect the results without bias to prove or disprove the theory. We may find we have to modify our theory based on the evidence collected and retest the revised theory.

Once our experiments have either supported or disproved our theory, the next step is to "publish" our research results to tell others exactly how we tested our theory and the results. This is to see if others can replicate the results using the same or equivalent alternative methods.

This book is a publication of theories about the nature of reality in the Spirit and Divine realms and methods to verify them labeled "Western Tantra." The main theory of Western Tantra is that the Universe is conscious, sentient, and cares what we do, and the practice of Western Tantra provides the methods we can use to transform ourselves into an instrument that can verify that. The principal method used on the Path of Ethics is to become a human that cares even more deeply about others.

⚔ THE BODY OF KNOWLEDGE: Before we begin, I will make a few comments about the existing body of human knowledge. We know a lot about the laws of nature, but much of this knowledge was gained with great difficulty by people with special skills. We call them Experts. We ordinary people do not replicate their experiments; rather we rely on other respected Experts with the same special skills to use their own methods to confirm their results. For example, I have not verified the speed of light myself nor how it bends with gravity. The scientists who have developed and confirmed the theories of light, gravity, evolution, and such have usually spent over ten thousand hours of training, over five years of full-time study, to be able to do what they do. Over twenty thousand hours would be more typical. For some, it is a lifetime of work. We do not personally verify every single thing they learn, but rather we put it in the body of human knowledge and rely on this knowledge to guide us. There is a word used to describe people who don't use this body of hard-won human knowledge. The word is ignorant.

It should be the same for the body of knowledge in the Spirit and Divine realms of knowledge. Some of us have spent tens of thousands of hours studying and experiencing worlds that take tens of thousands of hours to learn to access. I know I have. We then contact others who have devoted similar time to the hidden realms, and we ask them if their results are similar in this specialized area of knowledge. We then teach others or publish our results for people who do not have tens of thousands of hours to devote to acquiring this knowledge from raw data and trial and error. We hope that people will benefit if they try techniques we have developed in our specialized field of knowledge. In the dark and hidden spiritual-knowledge fields, our problem is that respected experts in the scientific fields ask us to prove our assertions of reality with results they can see without having done the inner work that is required to verify our results. That is equivalent to an untrained person asking a physicist to show that gravity bends light using a flashlight and a lead weight. Or asking a biologist to demonstrate with only the naked eye that DNA and RNA build proteins.

It is true that a biologist could show some steps in the process to a non-biologist with a microscope. But there is a problem with the unseen realms, because we first need to build a microscope that lets us see the unseen. It is possible to do this, but it takes some work by the would-be observer. How? What is the problem and how do we do it?

The problem is this: all our body's sensory organs and all our scientific measuring apparatus rely on ordinary matter and energy, especially the electromagnetic energy band, to register on our sensors. You may say only matter and energy exist, so if something has no mass or energy, then nothing is there, right? No, not really. We know that time and space exist, but these cannot register on our sensors except by their effects on ordinary matter and energy. Science has only positively identified about five percent of the matter present in our universe. From observations of this universe, scientists can calculate the approximate mass and diameter of our universe but can see only a small percentage of what *must* be there. Based on the movement of the galaxies, cosmologists believe another twenty-five percent or so of the mass of the universe must be matter that they cannot see, which they call "dark matter." Many scientists are trying to identify this dark matter, but as of this writing, scientists do not know what it is. So far, visible and dark matter combined only account for about thirty percent of what must be out there. The remaining seventy percent or so of stuff that *must* be there they call "dark energy," and scientists do not even have accepted theories about this seventy percent of what makes up the known universe. And that is just the known universe that we live in. If one of the various multiverse theories is correct, there may be a large or infinite number of other universes filling all space or creating other space-time.

It gets worse. The theories of quantum mechanics are among the most accurate known, predicting the results of some experiments to more than ten decimal places of accuracy. The mathematics of the promising string theories, which may unify quantum mechanics with relativity, require that our universe have at least ten dimensions. However we only see four dimensions, the three dimensions of our familiar space and one dimension of time. So there may be six or more additional dimensions that exist, but we cannot see them with our four dimensional sensory organs and scientific instruments. We may be prisoners in Plato's cave, only able to see a shadow world but not the higher dimensional world that creates it. Science has not proven the existence of these extra hidden dimensions, but these are serious theories that many scientists are now working on to confirm.

I believe that everything science has confirmed to be true *is* true, and our belief systems must be adjusted to be compatible with scientific findings. But we also need to remember that modern science is less than five hundred years old, and the age of the industrial revolution, which provides our modern scientific instruments, is about half that. That is only about four to ten human lifetimes to acquire what we currently know from science, compared to five thousand years of human records and tens of thousands of years of human existence. So if you ask whether science has discovered everything that exists, the answer has to be no; we are just getting started, and there is a long way to go. The best we can do right now is develop theories about what may lie in the vast unknown gaps in human knowledge.

Unfortunately we will not live long enough to know all the answers, so we have to go with what we know *now*. Can current science either prove or disprove the existence of an invisible creator deity or immortal conscious soul? No, science does not even know what consciousness is yet. Science *has* proven that about ninety-five percent of what *must* exist in our universe is currently invisible and unknown. Science does know that the five percent or so of ordinary matter-energy that we can see has evolved over time from a tiny homogeneous ball to the vast and complex universe we now see, including exceptionally complex sentient creatures that populate the earth. Science and our ordinary matter-energy sensors can see only the ordinary matter-energy world. What if space-time also evolved in complexity along with the matter-energy universe, and what if there could also be complex structures or even sentient beings in our universe constructed entirely out of time, space, or space-time? If these space-time complex structures have no matter-energy components, how would we see them? Our fledgling evolving science knows there is something in the universe expanding it and something holding the galaxies together; science just does not know what they are yet.

⚔ THEORIES: Does it matter? That depends on who and what we are. One of the things that science does not yet know is what consciousness is and where it is located. So far, all scientific efforts to even define it have failed. Because it currently eludes science's

matter-energy instruments, I am going to speculate that consciousness or the things that generate it may be made of the same mysterious multidimensional or dark matter-energy or pure space-time
stuff that is currently unknown. So what-science-does-not-yet-
know may be what we are, and the characteristics of this unknown
stuff may define our present existence and future fate. Let's see if
this idea leads to something we can test and verify.

Western Tantra will call this unknown stuff the Dark or
Darkness, and the instruments we need to explore the Dark world
may be inside us in the form of our own consciousness. Made of
the same Dark stuff, our consciousness may be able to illuminate
the Darkness. Western Tantra will call the sentient aspect of consciousness Heart-Mind and the entity made of unknown stuff
Soul, the core and essence of our being. Fortunately, humans have
been exploring the source and nature of consciousness for over five
thousand years, ten times longer than our scientific body of knowledge, so we do not need to start from scratch to develop a theory
of the Soul.

Scientists may say that because Dark stuff cannot be measured,
there is no way to test the theory of Soul, and it is beyond the
realm of science. Not so. Every one of us will test one aspect of
the theory, that the Soul survives the death of the Body. Strong
evidence exists that our bodies will die, and many of us have personally witnessed bodies die. When each of us dies we will either
experience consciousness continuing after the death of our body
or we will not. The results are definite and repeatable by anyone,
although the results are difficult to describe to anyone who has not
yet done the experiment.

I was once an atheist and held the opinion that when we
died, our consciousness did not continue. My logic, based on the
assumption that consciousness was generated by the brain, said

this had to be so. The data point I used was that if an afterlife and enduring soul existed, and if a person temporarily died, as defined by lack of brain activity, and was later brought back with medical intervention, then the person should be able to recall the afterlife when revived. Because I had heard of no such experiences, I concluded there is no afterlife or enduring soul. Turns out I was wrong. Not only are there abundant accounts of an afterlife from those who have had temporary death experiences, there are also numerous accounts of people remembering prior lives and an afterlife (or time between lives) by people who reincarnated after permanent death experiences, and some of these people could validate prior lives. Some advanced meditators seem to be able to view and describe other times and places while their body remains in a trance-like state. To hear these accounts all you have to do is listen with an open mind to what others report. It helps not to call them crazy or liars. Just saying.

When I checked out my own vivid dreams of events in prior times and found the events actually happened, it blew my "one-life-and-when-we-are-dead-we-no-longer-exist" theory all to hell, and I had to come up with a new theory about how reality works. I'm not trying to convince you of anything. I'm just describing what happened to me. If you want to learn what I learned, you have to do your own work with your own tools.

We are flawed creatures with limited knowledge. A theory is what seems to best fit the data one has collected, and the theory must be checked out and changed if results conflict. Although the theories of reality described here are almost certainly wrong in some respects and will have to be modified, they also seem to work. Not to undersell my work too much, the theories are based on well over twenty thousand hours of Tibetan Buddhist Tantric training, well over twenty thousand hours of Buddhist meditation, well over twenty thousand hours of conventional advanced education in the sciences, and more decades of life experience than I care to admit. So what follows are theories about the way things are, which we will call Western Tantric philosophy.

HOMEWORK:

1. On paper make three columns. In the first column, list all the things you believe about the nature of this universe, our nature and place in it, and divine nature or lack of it. In the second column, after each belief, list the basis of that belief and where the belief came from. In the third column, list what you did to verify that the belief is true. So for example, if you wrote in the first column that the world is round, then in the next column you would put where you got this information, and in the third column you would describe that you flew or cruised around the world traveling west or east and ended up back at your starting location.

2. From the above table, pick out one or two critically important items that you have not personally verified, such as "when we die we go to heaven." Develop a plan to verify what you think is correct.

FURTHER READING:

There are many fine books describing the current efforts by Western science to understand the universe we live in. Suggested authors include Stephen Hawking, Michio Kaku, Lisa Randall, and others. My recommendation for catching up with the "bleeding edge" of physics and cosmology is *The Elegant Universe* by

Brian Greene, which includes string and brane theory up to 2008. For more recent developments, including the Higgs particle and gravity waves, I suggest subscribing to *Science News* (www.sciencenews.org) to stay current with the latest developments in all the branches of Western science and medicine.

CHAPTER 4

WESTERN TANTRIC PHILOSOPHY

"It is now time, leaving every object of the sense far behind,
to contemplate, by a certain ascent, a
beauty of a much higher order;
a beauty not visible to the corporeal eye, but alone manifest
to the brighter eye of the soul, independent of all corporeal aid."

—PLOTINUS, *AN ESSAY ON THE BEAUTIFUL*

I n the philosophy of Western Tantra, our true nature is consciousness, pure awareness, and that consciousness endures beyond the
life of our body. All conscious beings are made of the same stuff,
whatever that is. Our true nature we call Soul or True Self. Soul
seems to have a source of consciousness energy called Prana, Inner
Fire, Chi, Qi, Ki, Kundalini, Power, Mana, Medicine, Juju, Life
Force, Breath, Light, and other names. Many spiritual systems
divide this energy into two flavors, often called female and male

energy, yin and yang. This energy feels like Love and may be Love, but we will mainly call it Energy or Life Force.

By nature and nurture we create a plan for interacting with our surroundings, especially with other people. We will call this our Ego, Personality, or False Self. It is our false self-concept because we think it is our true nature, but it is merely a persona or character we create, a fiction. Our False Self often includes objects like clothes, cars, and homes; other people like family, friends, groups, and heroes; as well as belief systems, locations, names and titles. But especially, False Self includes our human body. All this serves to identify each of us, both to ourselves and to others. Intended to protect us from harm, Ego also separates us from others, seeing ourselves as different from others, better or worse in different traits.

Ego is a thought concept and cannot use ordinary energy, so it must maintain itself with consciousness Energy from the Soul. Because it is a non-physical creation and is fed by the Soul, Ego can outlive the Body. But because Ego separates itself from others, including God (the rest of the Universe), Ego prevents us from achieving our ultimate potential, full union with Reality. So over-coming Ego is the chief aim of many spiritual techniques.

Remember that Western Tantric philosophy is a set of theories about the way things are, as stated in the prior chapter. To accept this philosophy as True, you should apply these ideas and methods to your life, to see if they make your life better and better explain what you experience. In other words, test these theories with your own life experiments.

THE UNIVERSE IS MOSTLY UNKNOWN. We are part of the universe and made of the same stuff. We are conscious, sentient, and care what happens to us. The universe is at least partly conscious and sentient because it includes us; we are part of it.

Some say that consciousness is an integral aspect of the physical information that defines systems, fundamental particles, and fields; thus the entire universe by this definition is conscious. If consciousness is a fundamental property of the known universe, this suggests that consciousness is conserved, just as physical information is conserved. Conservation means it cannot be destroyed, only separated into its fundamental parts and rearranged to create new systems. Sentience may be defined as how well information is integrated; thus large portions of the universe may be sentient (Christof Koch, *Consciousness*, 132). As a minimum, we know that humanity, our part of the known universe, is sentient and at least that part cares what happens to us. An extreme view is that the entire Universe is the mind of God that cares deeply about all of us. Reality may lie between these extremes.

Our sentient consciousness is our Soul, which is at least partly within our Body but outlives the Body, and therefore must be able to leave the Body when the Body dies and dissolves into its component parts. An extreme view is that Soul is completely separate from the Body and can leave at will. Another extreme view is that Soul does not exist at all. Reality may lie between these extreme views, with the Soul related to the Body in some way but able to detach under some conditions.

Like everything else in the known universe, Souls must evolve and, like every creature on earth, they must mature. Because Souls may outlive the Body, Body age and Soul age may differ. There could be Souls living their first human lives in old bodies and old Souls having lived multiple lives now in young Bodies. This could account for child prodigies who seem to come into their lives with skills beyond what is typical of children. It could even account for adults who have mental or physical abilities far beyond those of normal adults. This creates a problem when testing such things as healing or psychic abilities. If these abilities are part of the Soul, then we cannot assume that all people have special abilities in equal measure, or that some special abilities relate to the maturity of the physical Body when matching subjects for experiments. It is also a mistake to view any human as superior to another because of special abilities. Their Souls may only be at a different stage of spiritual development, just as ten-year-old children are not seen as superior to five-year-olds. The older children have just been around longer and can do things the younger children will be able to do when they are the same age. Spiritual maturity may work the same way. This could explain why some people display great humanity while others in genetically similar bodies act more like animals.

When we live within physical human bodies, we live individual realities separated from other humans' experiences. Living within human bodies, our reality is what happens after our sensory apparatus and nervous system impulses project into the human brain. For example, photons from our outer world pass through the lenses of our eyes onto light sensitive cells in our retinas, which send electrochemical nerve impulses to neurons in the visual cortex of our brain. Associative neurons in our brain assign meaning to the sensory nerve impulses, based on our past history, and construct a representation of outer reality within the brain. Every person's interior brain representation of outer reality is different from every other person's reality because of the different associations within each person's brain, based on their unique past history. For us, there is no uniform, objective outer reality. It is always colored by our past associations.

So for example, one person seeing a black man approaching might have mental associations with criminals and experience fear, while another person standing next to the fearful person may have mental associations of friend, family, protector, or pastor, and experience joy as the very same man approaches. The two people are experiencing very different realities from the same outer events. Yet we make authoritative pronouncements about our outer environment as if our perceptions were objective reality. We say Joe is an asshole and Jane is a saint, as if these were fixed attributes of Joe and Jane that are inherently part of them. In reality, if you see an asshole, the asshole must be located within your own brain; otherwise you will not be able to associate the photons and sounds arriving from an outer world as matching your own inner asshole. The same goes for perceptions of saintliness. It takes one to know one, as they say.

There is no objective outer reality. We all have different inner experiences of outer reality based on our unique inner associations, based in turn on our different histories. I think we can take this as a given and not bother proving it. However if you disagree, try having some arguments with your spouse, lover, teenager, or boss, and see if their interpretation of reality matches yours.

⚜ REALITY: In the more esoteric world of Western Tantra, reality is an interrelated subjective totality, a unity, but can be thought of as having three aspects, a triune reality. The first of the three is the ordinary material reality that we all see and accept to some degree, including the ordinary energy that runs this world. We call this the Material world or the Material Form realm. We often think that only material reality is "real" because we can see it and touch it, and other people of the same background seem to agree that what we see is what they see. What we do not realize is how much, if not all, of material reality depends on concepts and thoughts to make it real. For example, you may be sitting on a chair. You think the chair is objectively a chair and has fixed, inherent reality as a chair. In truth, the chair as you perceive it would not exist if some designer had not conceived of that chair and some makers had not brought the component parts of the chair together to form the designer's idea of a chair. We then label it a "chair" because it has a culturally determined shape and it keeps our butt from hitting the floor. In other words, it functions as our concept of chair. In a different culture, the same object in their world might be an altar or firewood.

The dreams and plans and ideas that create the physical reality we see around us are the second essential part of our reality and must be considered "real," even if we can't see or touch these ideas. We will call this imaginary world or world of thoughts, words, concepts, dreams, and visions the Spirit world or Spirit Form realm. Our plan for interacting with the Material world, which is our self-concept or Ego, belongs to this world of thought. If the Mind of God is defined as the set of physical laws that make up this universe, then every part of our universe was thought into existence by the words of God. In the beginning was the Word, and the Word was with God, and the Word was God (John 1:1).

But what produces the forms we perceive in the Spirit realm? Where do the words, plans, thoughts, and dreams originate? The spiritual, religious, and philosophical literature calls this source of forms the Formless realm, Pure Potential, or the Source. This is the third essential part of reality. Artists perceive the Formless as the well from which spring their ideas, and marvel that it never seems to run dry. Everything that could exist lives here, so this realm also has reality as potential reality. With my limited knowledge of quantum mechanics, it is my understanding that when doing experiments with fundamental particles, one must account for every possible path a particle could take, so potential seems to have a reality or existence. Possibly the quantum amplitude or wave function that reveals where a particle can appear may be part of this Formless realm. Remember that I guaranteed that not everything here is correct, but please do not throw out everything written here because of a few mistakes. Because our consciousness has never been located but we know it exists, Western Tantra will assign our consciousness to the Formless realm. Concepts of an invisible, formless supreme being also belong here, so the Formless can also be called the Divine realm. The Spirit realm that acts as an intermediary bringing the Formless into Form can therefore be called the Middle realm.

So these are the three aspects of reality in Western Tantra: the Material world, the Spirit or Middle realm, and the Formless realm of pure potential. Remember that Western Tantra defines God or Reality or Totality as the entire universe and everything that is, could be, or ever could have been, seen and unseen. Thus God can also be thought of as a trinity with a Material aspect reflecting Divinity, such as Jesus, the prophets, saints, or teachers; a Formless aspect, referred to as the Father, Yahweh, The Nameless, Emptiness, Voidness and other terms; and finally a Spirit aspect acting as an intermediary, bringing the Formless into Form, variously termed Holy Ghost, Sophia, the goddess, angels, buddhas and other terms. Similarly, a person can be thought to have a Material Body, a Formless Soul, and an Ego or Spirit that acts as an intermediary between the Material Body and the Formless Soul. All the realms interrelate, and all are part of Totality, which technically cannot be subdivided. But to go further, we need to choose a theory to test and a realm in which to do our work. So for this book of *Western Tantra*, we will do our work mostly in the Material realm, the Real world, and test the theory that there is a God or Ultimate Reality consisting of a conscious universe or multiverse that cares about us.

✂ TRIUNE PATHS: A set of techniques to reach Ultimate Reality is typically referred to as a Path, and we will call seeking Ultimate Reality in the Real world *The White Path of Ethics*. In Buddhism, white symbolizes skillful means and the energy center located in the head, so the shorthand "White Path" will distinguish this Path from *The Red Path of Meditation* working in the Spirit realm and *The Blue Path of Union* working in the Formless realm. It is an interesting coincidence that the Buddhist colors symbolizing the energy centers Western Tantra works with in the head, throat, and heart are the same white, red, and blue colors found in the flags of many Western nations, symbolizing the qualities of those nations.

All three Paths that we use in Western Tantra have the same three principal aspects: Love, Renunciation, and Wisdom. Just as each Path works mainly in one of the three realms, each Path also concentrates mainly on one principal aspect. *The White Path of Ethics* emphasizes Love, *The Red Path of Meditation* concentrates more on Renunciation, and *The Blue Path of Union* focuses mainly on Wisdom. However all three principal aspects are used to a greater or lesser degree in all three Paths. All three Paths lead to the same result in different ways, reaching one's ultimate potential as a human. If *The White Path of Ethics* emphasizing Love as the principal aspect of the Path is not for you, then try one of the other Western Tantric Paths or the Path of an entirely different spiritual system. There are as many Paths to Ultimate Reality as there are different types of people. Here are the three principal aspects of all Tantric Paths.

✂ LOVE: Unconditional love is something everyone wants from others, and some people want universal love for all others. What do you do if you do not feel that kind of love? If your love is conditional, loving others only if they make you feel good, or if you have love only for a select few, then how do you get this kind of love? First let's be sure we know what universal and unconditional love are. Universal means for everyone and everything. Unconditional means without any exceptions, assumptions, fine print, or if-then clauses such as: if you will love me, then I will love you. Together, universal and unconditional love make up Divine Love, the Love a sentient Universe has for all of creation, God's Love for all beings. This is the love we need in order to become one with the Universe, to experience Totality. We will use the concept of universal unconditional Divine Love a lot in this book, so we will just call it Love, capitalized.

This Love is lovely to get but hard to give. If you have never seen this kind of Love, watch the movie *Casablanca* or get a dog. Developing the capacity for Love begins with a wish. It is hard to create something in yourself that you do not really want, and you can be sure your Ego does not want universal unconditional Love for others, just self-love with conditions. The Ego life plan wants everyone to love Ego unconditionally, but will give love subject only to Ego's terms and conditions. Ego wants to be treated in a particular way at certain times and to be free to do whatever it wants to do with its lovers. Who would not love someone who became their servant and made them feel like royalty? Unfortunately the lover's Ego wants the same treatment, and it is hard to be a servant and feel like royalty. So people with strong Egos seldom get the love they are looking for.

Fortunately, we all have within us a Soul that is part of the Universe and is already in Love with all-that-is. We just need to find our Heart and connect it with Reality. One Tantric method for doing this is to visualize what we want to become, and then act as if we have already achieved it.

That is where community service work is especially valuable. You can help or work with strangers who may be different from you. At first you may be indifferent to those you are helping, but as you learn that those you help are as human as you, and as you act as if you care what you are doing, your thoughts will align with what your Body is doing and saying. You will begin to actually care. At some point you will be struck by someone's plight or story, and your Heart will begin to open; you will actually feel their emotional state, something from which we generally protect ourselves. Opening the Heart is dropping the boundary or wall between yourself and others.

Next bring this openness home and see how unique and special the people in your life are and what they add to your life in good times and bad. Love them in your Heart without asking for anything in return, even those who seem to hate and disrespect you. Yes teenagers, I'm looking at you.

Finally, bring this openness and Love back to yourself. Look at all the parts of you that you used to dislike, and Love all of you, warts and all, including the parts your Ego ignored, hated, or pretended they belonged to others, as if they were not parts of you. Only the open Heart of Love which is part of Totality can Love totally. Look at yourself, what you have become as a human being and imagine the Love of the Universe that shaped you. Realize that Love. Become that Love. Share that Love with others.

✂ RENUNCIATION: The Western Tantric practitioner relies on experience and evidence, not opinions and belief. Numerous religious writings notwithstanding, there is no evidence that we can take our current body or any other material possessions into the next life. All things Material degrade and decay with time except maybe for a few subatomic particles, at least until the collapse or tearing asunder of our current universe. There is nothing in the Material world that will preserve your physical body or your material possessions forever. Not doctors nor hospitals nor houses nor money nor guns nor laws will do anything but delay the inevitable. Even the Earth and Sun and the physical universe we live in will die eventually. Sorry.

For this reason, the Tantric practitioner renounces the Material as a solution for most problems and looks to the spiritual for the pathway to the eternal. On the Path of Ethics, this does not mean you must give away everything and live like a hermit. On this Path we are doing our work in the Real world, but we do not rely on the Material for salvation. Instead we stop clinging to Material things and stop thinking that possessions or money bring happiness, and we renounce personal Material gain.

Instead, we turn our Material assets and advantages into Karma that we can use in the life after this one. We do this by using our physical life to work for the benefit of others, to help everyone in any way possible, retaining only what we need to sustain our own physical lives. In this way we develop loving relationships with others and awaken the Heart, which can form a relationship with God, Totality, the Universe, or however you like to view your home in the eternal beyond this life.

✂ WISDOM: When referring to a spiritual Path, Wisdom means understanding how Reality works. Nothing exists on its own, independent of the rest of the universe. Energy, matter, time and space all arise and evolve in dependence on unwritten laws of the universe which determine how all parts of the universe form, interact, and function. No object or concept possesses any inherent existence or characteristics independent of the rest of creation. All things and concepts exist in dependence on causes and conditions. All aspects of reality interpenetrate. For example, matter has space and an energy equivalence, and affects space and time in accordance with unwritten relationships that can be described in words and numbers by scientific laws.

Scientifically speaking, if something were to take away the universe, everything in it would also disappear; nothing in the universe exists on its own. Even time and space depend on the total universe and all its interrelations. Similarly, you cannot extract a person from the world without the causes and conditions that formed the person's physical body or the concepts that defined the person. The person's body requires a mother and father and the Earth and Sun, all of which were made over time from exploding stars. The concepts that describe the person depend on the society surrounding the person. Nothing is independent of its time or surroundings. There is only an interdependent whole called Totality, and everything we do affects everything else.

Because we are not fixed, independent entities with inherent characteristics, we can change our relationships with other humans and with the Divine. If we have Wisdom, if we understand how things exist, interrelate, and transform, we can become better and help others better.

HOMEWORK:

1. If you do not already have unconditional Love for everyone and everything, start the steps found in the section on Love above. Use journaling to record your progress.

2. If you have a spiritual tradition with a trinity, see if *Triune Reality* helps explain it.

FURTHER READING:

It is not an easy read, but if you want to know more about the scientific exploration into the nature of consciousness based on information theory, and why the entire universe may be conscious, then read *Consciousness* by Christof Koch.

CHAPTER 5

THE CIRCLE OF KARMA

"The power of the world always works in circles. . . ."
—BLACK ELK, *BLACK ELK SPEAKS*

M ost of the White Path Tantric techniques we will use here depend on the concept of Karma, the law of Cause and Effect. Simply put, if you want to experience a particular effect, you must first generate the cause that produces that effect. In general, this means you must give what you want to receive. What goes around comes around.

To Westerners, this seems counter-intuitive, illogical. If I want something, it means I don't have it. How can I give what I don't have? The Western way is to ask for what we want, and if we don't get it ask louder, and if we still don't get what we want, make deals or get angry and demand it and make threats, and maybe even take it with force. This seems like a direct way to get what we want: just ask, deal, demand, or take. Logic says we should get what we ask for.

Karma says if you plead you will get pleas, if you demand you will get demands, if you threaten you will get threats, if you use anger you will get back anger, and if you use force you will be attacked. Sometimes people give what is asked, and often there is a lag between what we give out and what we receive in return, which fools people into thinking the demanding approach works. For example, thieves demand money at gunpoint, scaring victims and getting money, but then live their lives in fear and later police catch them and take the money away. They gave fear and got back fear. They took money and money was taken from them. They made someone poor and were made poor.

A lot of life is cyclic. For example, we leave home and go to work and then return home again. So we leave for work, a motorist cuts us off, we get angry and give them the one-finger salute, they get offended and angry, and we think (logically) that we scored a victory. But life is cyclic. The angry motorist makes other motorists angry, they take it out at work, and when we return home, we drive with a bunch of pissed-off motorists who are rude and make us angry on the way home. We gave out anger and received anger in return, but it happened in a cycle and the connection is not always obvious.

You have probably been demanding or asking for what you want all your life, so you probably do not have to try this method again. Just ask yourself, "How is that working out for me so far?" If you are getting everything you want, then fine, keep it up. If not, try giving others what you want for yourself. So the next time your spouse or partner gets angry at you, but you really want love and kindness, give love and kindness and keep doing that. Remember: life is cyclic and it may take time to get back what you give. There may be a lot of past anger in the circle that may have to unload on you first. That is why people have trouble perceiving Cause and Effect. There may be a long lag time before you get back what you give.

Also remember that it is not all about you getting what you want. Focus on giving to others and do not think at all about getting anything in return. The Ego is the part of us that wants for itself, and because Ego sees us as separate from God, from intimate contact with Reality, we want to avoid feeding the Ego too much. Eventually we want to transform our Ego into a more effective life plan and (hopefully) eventually get rid of it completely, becoming selfless.

KARMA AND TANTRA: Karmic practice is giving what you want to receive. A related Tantric practice is to "Be what you want to become." This is similar to the familiar Western technique that lets underlings become managers by acting like a manager in order to become one, or whatever position they are trying to fill. The difference with Tantra is that we emulate an Enlightened Being, a person who is one with Reality or God as defined here.

So what are the characteristics of one who is in tune with Reality? Reality is interconnected; all beings are part of the whole. So if any person or creature is in pain, all of interconnected Reality experiences that pain. It follows that all Reality prefers pleasure to pain and cares about whatever the different parts of Reality experience, just as your interconnected Body cares about the pain of a smashed thumb and prefers the pleasure generated by your genitals.

To emulate an Enlightened Being, care about all parts of reality. You do not need to be told to attend to a smashed thumb; you do it quickly and spontaneously. Its pain is your pain. So it is with people and other creatures. When you see any person or creature in pain, try to help as best you can. If you give help, you will get help, which improves your chances of becoming Enlightened. When you see anyone experiencing joy, rejoice in their good fortune. Let their joy be your joy. This is especially beneficial during sex with a partner, as we will see later.

Although the Ego prevents direct contact with another's feelings, the human brain at least has an empathy circuit that will help you emulate what others are feeling. So to emulate a loving Reality, be aware of people and creatures around you and help them experience pleasure and mitigate pain in any way possible, within your skills and resources. Yes, this does mean you will have to stop deliberately squashing bugs that are not harming you. But it does not mean you have to become a vegetarian; after all plants are also conscious, living things in Western Tantric philosophy. It does mean you have to start caring about how your food is treated, as Native Americans used to respect and care for the living things that gave their lives to sustain them, including the living Mother Earth. Wasted food, water, and energy, and fouled air are among the crimes committed by Westerners.

✄ KARMA'S FRUIT: Intent to harm or help is key to the results you will experience. Not every altruistic act will be appreciated nor will every intent to harm come back to bite you in this life. It is a circle or cycle, like a crop cycle. You will reap what you sow, and only what you plant will you harvest. But the crop will not spring up immediately, maybe not until a future life. And the mysterious weeds or flowers that appear in your current life may have grown from seeds that were there before you were born.

The Universe helps others without expecting reward or gratitude, in fact we curse the Universe for our misfortune more often than we express gratitude. In the same way we must act without expecting reward or praise, because as it says in the Christian New Testament, if we act for praise, then we have already received our reward (Matthew 6:2). So help all others all the time without any expectation of reward and see what happens.

It may take a while to see any results, but if you persist and pay attention, you should see two things start to happen. First, by the law of Karma, if you make life better for others, you should experience life getting better for yourself. Secondly, if you are persistent in helping others, the conscious, sentient Universe should notice that you are starting to help it help others and begin to help you help others. A sentient Universe would be pretty stupid if it did not help you help its children. As your mind begins to match Universal Mind, you begin to synchronize with the flow of Reality and notice that fortuitous events seem to aid your efforts in ways not explained by chance.

One example often expressed by people who are on a spiritual path is "parking karma." As the West becomes more crowded and more prosperous, most Western adults have cars, and in some places there are more cars than parking spaces. Most Westerners have experienced orbiting a block or parking lot looking for a space. This often takes time and patience. A strange phenomenon seems to occur when one has been consistently helping others and is currently driving somewhere to help someone. When on a mission to help others, parking spaces seem to appear at just the right time and place to facilitate helping others. As you pull up to the clinic with your sick friend, another car is pulling out right where you need to be. For someone used to orbiting a block for ten minutes to find parking, this feels like a miracle. Maybe it is a miracle.

✄ MIRACLES: Maybe we need to rethink what a miracle is. Atheists seem to think miracles are impossible events, and scientists and skeptics seem to think miracles are events with no natural explanation. I think impossible events are actually impossible and only natural events can occur. By the definition of God that we are exploring, God is the entire universe and all that exists, including the natural laws that define what can occur in the universe. So by this definition, impossible things cannot exist and only natural events can occur in the universe.

Requiring miracles to be impossible or to violate the natural laws of the universe is the same as defining miracles as events that can never happen, so by definition, if something happens, then it is not a miracle. The word then becomes useless, applying to nothing in the Real world.

But is this the actual definition or what people mean when they describe a miracle? I think not. *Webster's* defines "miracle" as an extremely outstanding or unusual event, thing, or accomplishment, or an extraordinary event manifesting a supernatural work of God. So for Western Tantra, we will define Miracle as a natural occurrence that is either so rare or so improbable in its timing and beneficial in its outcome that it suggests the presence of Divine intervention. So for example, we know that quantum tunneling is a rare but possible natural event, but if it occurs at the exact microsecond needed to save Schrodinger's cat from death, then it is a Miracle by the definition used here, even though every part of the event is possible and completely natural (except for putting a poor cat in a box with a radioactive source to release a lethal poison, you sick bastards).

Let's try out this new definition of Miracle on an event described in the Christian New Testament (Acts 9:1-20). A guy named Saul of Tarsus was traveling the road to Damascus and had a vision of Jesus Christ that blinded him. This was after the Crucifixion, and Saul was on his way to hunt down and judge Christians, which in those days meant killing them. For three days Saul remained in Damascus sick and blind, probably seeing physicians of that era to no avail. In the city, a Christian named Ananias had a dream or vision of Jesus telling him to go to the house where Saul was and heal him. Ananias probably said something in Assyrian or Aramaic loosely translated as, "Are you shitting me Lord? That guy came here to kill us!" But the vision of Jesus said he needed Saul for a mission and to do as he said, so Ananias went to the house and laid hands on Saul, telling him Jesus commanded him to restore Saul's sight. Then things like scales fell from Saul's eyes and he could see again. Saul changed his name to Paul and became the messenger of Jesus to the gentiles, writing most of the New Testament in the process.

Paul's vision of Jesus and the restoration of his sight are recognized by established Christian religions as miracles. Atheists might say this story is impossible. Scientists and skeptics might say the events violate natural laws, and using Occam's razor, might conclude that the whole story is a lie designed to promote Christianity.

Let's now analyze this story using Western science and Western Tantra's definition of Miracle. I am a health and safety professional with a master's degree in safety and over fifty years of education and experience in health and safety. First, what probably happened on the road to Damascus? They were crossing a desert, and we know that the sun reflecting off sand can have the same effect as off snow and can cause snow blindness, in which the optic nerves produce light flashes and the cornea is damaged by the sun's ultraviolet rays and becomes opaque, resulting in blindness. Dehydration can cause hallucinations. Moving sand can create sounds like voices. So all of the eyewitness accounts on the road to Damascus are not only possible by natural laws, but are also probable. There is no reason to attribute this to lying or mythology. It is more likely that the witnesses were describing actual events than assuming they all were lying, so Occam's razor is satisfied by the Biblical account of what happened on the road.

What about the faith healing? The cornea self-heals after sun damage, and in a few days the damaged cell layers of the cornea slough off and vision returns. Knowing human nature, it is probable that Saul's knowing that the people he came to kill were the same ones who came to cure him would cause Saul to tear up, washing away the dead cornea cells which would look like opaque contact lenses or, to that era, fish scales. So these events described by eyewitnesses are also probable, and there is no reason to discount the Biblical account on the basis of natural laws.

As to the internal events of visions and dreams, we know hallucinations and dreams can occur naturally, and our internal worlds can influence our outer behavior, so there is no reason to doubt that a guy thinking of killing Christians would have an hallucination about Christ, or that a Christian would know in what house a Christian killer is located, or that a Christian would have a dream or vision that Christ would want him to love his enemy and try to heal him. Nothing in the thoughts or actions of the people in this story is impossible or out of character. So thinking scientifically and skeptically, everything in this story could be explained by natural laws and coincidence, right?

Well let's look at the Western Tantric definition of Miracle again. A Miracle is defined here as a natural occurrence that is either so rare or so improbable in its timing and so beneficial in its outcome that it suggests the presence of Divine intervention. Nothing in the Damascus story required exceptionally rare events. If you need proof, read up on dreams, hallucinations, snow blindness, and singing sands. Everything in the story could have happened as stated, so rarity does not qualify the events as a Miracle. But what about the timing?

Let's look at the timing. Getting sun damage causing blindness and hallucinations in the desert: probable. Ananias feeling compelled to help an enemy in accordance with Christ's lessons and knowing where a Christian-killer is located: probable. No Miracles yet.

What about Ananias arriving at Saul's side at the exact moment when Saul's tears would wash away the damaged corneas? If Saul's eyes had recovered before Ananias had arrived, Saul would likely have thought God had restored his sight in time to catch another Christian, and he would have continued condemning Christians to death for their heresy. If Ananias had left with Saul still blind, Saul may have given him points for trying but would not likely have become the Apostle Paul, author of the Epistles and converter of the gentiles. Without Paul's conversion, most likely we gentiles in the West would never have heard of Jesus Christ.

So does this count as a Miracle? A series of complex natural events most likely occurred which individually were all possible, but collectively were so improbable in their timing that had they not occurred in just that way, we would not today know of the teachings of Jesus Christ. So yes, this was a series of events so improbable in their timing and so beneficial in their outcome that it suggests the influence of a Divine consciousness, exquisite in its timing and knowledge of natural law and human behavior.

To me, this was a Miracle. This from a guy who used to be an atheist who subscribed to the *Skeptical Inquirer* magazine and its philosophy. The point of understanding Miracles is that we want to be able to spot them when they happen, building our confidence in the possibility that the Universe may be conscious, sentient, and cares about us.

HERE ARE EXAMPLES from my life about spotting Miracles as they occur. One of the problems in my safety profession is that if you do your job well, nothing happens. After doing my job for years, I was having trouble believing that I was saving lives or even benefiting others. In that state of mind, one year when I was Christmas shopping in San Francisco's Union Square, I saw a homeless man sleeping on a sheet of cardboard with no coat or blanket in temperature that was close to freezing. I knew I had some old sleeping bags at home and that homeless people froze to death on the streets every year in the San Francisco bay area. So I decided I would start giving sleeping bags and warm clothing to homeless people on the streets when the weather turned cold every year, knowing that if I did this enough times, I would save at least one life and make others more comfortable.

After doing this a few years with no intention of giving up, I noticed that lucky coincidences started making helping others easier. One year my helpers and I were given a carload of socks, and we happened to find a group passing out a truck full of shoes to the homeless. A minor Miracle.

Another winter we happened to spot a sick homeless woman who had just been discharged from a hospital. She led us to her homeless encampment, which had just been stripped of its tents and blankets by a road maintenance crew that day while the group was away at a soup kitchen getting dinner. What the fuck is wrong with the people who ordered and executed the removal of shelter from the homeless and the hospital staff who discharged an old sick woman with no place to go? We gave out our entire carload of donated warm clothing to the woman and her encampment on the eve of what was to be the coldest night of that winter, a major Miracle in its timing, probably saving lives.

The group that helped me pass out warm clothing and bedding most years was the Tse Chen Ling Buddhist center in San Francisco. The founding lama, Lama Zopa Rinpoche, recommended I study

Lam Rim, so I became the teaching assistant to the two teachers who taught that course there. The second Lam Rim teacher had been a successful drug and alcohol counselor but fell off the wagon in the traumatic aftermath of the 9/11 World Trade Center collapse. One evening he failed to show up to teach the class, and his friends and students at the center were worried about him. Some said they had earlier received no answer from his phone or the doorbell of his second story gated apartment. This was before cell phones were common.

For some reason, I was the only one available to look for him by car, and all I had to go by was his address and a paper map. This was before GPS was available. I had never been to his apartment, so I tried to memorize the map. I started out into the dark. Fog and darkness kept me from reading street signs or the map, and within minutes I was completely lost on roads that did not allow stopping. With no option but to allow intuition to guide me, I made turns by guess and feel. After driving blind for about four miles, I finally found a parking place where I could pull over and check my map. Finding a parking place in San Francisco is a Miracle in itself. It turned out this parking place was a block from my teacher's home, and I had arrived there by blind intuition.

I wondered how I was going to get in as I walked around the corner to his apartment, but as I approached, I saw him coming out of his apartment to get more booze at the liquor store near where I had parked. We greeted each other as if our meeting had been planned, walked together to the liquor store, and then I followed him into his apartment, where we talked for hours. What amazed me at the time, and even now, was this: all I had to do was have the intention to help my teacher and friend, and buddhas or angels or something guided me unerringly through four miles of darkness and fog to the doorstep of where I needed to be, at the one-and-only moment in time that evening that anyone would be able to check on him and report his status to his friends who wanted to help him. This was so improbable in its timing and beneficial in its outcome that I call this a Miracle. I could barely believe it was happening as the sequence of events unfolded at the time or even now as I remember it. I do not expect any readers to believe this account, although I swear it happened just this way.

I am not actually asking you to believe me at all. I am trying to convince you to try helping others in need, wherever you find them, and see what happens for yourself. I am hoping to awaken your curiosity. What if we are immortal beings and the Universe is sentient and actually cares about us and what we do? Would not that be really cool and worth checking out? How would you do that without having to die to find out? These ideas, persistently applied, inspired me. Maybe they will work for you too.

✂ ETHICAL ACTION IN THE REAL WORLD: Everyone helps others, but to be honest, most of the time we are helping ourselves. If you decide to try consistently helping everyone you can with whatever resources you have, here are some tips. The acts have to benefit people or other living things and be performed without expectation of reward. If you profit from any act in any way except personal satisfaction or transformation, then you have already been rewarded. Don't expect something miraculous to happen every time you do something to benefit another. Don't expect people you help to appreciate what you do for them. Most of the time they will not appreciate your help or will not notice; or they may feel it is their due or they may even resent your help. You are trying to please the sentient Universe, not yourself or the ones you try to help. But if you persistently do the work God would do if God were you, if you can act as if you are God's agent in the world without feeding your own Ego, if you are open-minded and attentive, then eventually you should see Miracles, evidence that the Universe cares what you are doing and is assisting you in ways that cannot be explained by chance.

Think of it this way: if God is the sentient Universe, then the only physical eyes, ears, arms, and legs God has to see and help others are yours and those of others. If everyone in the world kept only what they need and passed on the rest to someone in need, eventually everyone would have what they need to live. If you are careful not to hurt yourself or others physically or financially, the practice of helping others is harmless. Helping make the world a better place is not a waste of time, even if nothing happens to reveal God to you.

But if the Universe is sentient and cares about us, an intelligent Universe should notice who is sharing and helping and should provide signs that the helpers are noticed and appreciated. That is the first purpose of becoming an agent for God in the Material world, learning for yourself that the Universe is conscious and cares about us. Knowing that what the Mystics say may be true gives us confidence to begin the serious work of transforming ourselves from who we are now to our ultimate human potential.

⚜ IT'S NOT WORKING: What if you already work toward making the world better, even for years, and you have not seen evidence of God? There are several reasons why Reality would not reveal itself to you.

One possible reason may be an excessive dependence on a large altruistic Ego. You may be too heavily invested in seeing yourself as a good person who always helps others. The Ego is our life plan for interacting with our environment, and many people are very proud of who they are. However, all Ego structures are self-created images of ourselves as different from others, whether better or worse. This perceived difference puts a boundary between us and the rest of the universe, including God. The aim of most spiritual traditions is to become selfless, rather than any particular way we think we should be. In selflessness we can become part of God. So if you are too Ego-invested in being altruistic, the Universe may avoid feeding your Ego, not because your Ego is "bad" but because it separates your true nature from full contact with the Totality that is God. You should continue your altruistic work, but avoid seeking praise from any source; embrace criticism, and cultivate Love.

Another possible reason for not seeing God at work in the world may be that you hold concepts of God or Reality that are off the mark or are so cherished that true revelation would traumatize you by violating your beliefs, especially tightly held atheistic beliefs. For this you must cultivate an open mind and the courage to face whatever is true. Try to cultivate a sense of mystery, an acceptance that you will not have all the answers; whatever is revealed will be okay. Realize that our internal worlds are all unique and other faiths may see God differently. God may be revealed in a different form or method than what you are used to. Let go of attachment to cherished beliefs.

Another reason you may not see God at work is that you may not be paying close attention, or you may have refused aid because it did not appear in the way you were looking for. For example, say you run a community help center or spiritual center that is struggling to survive financially. A local drug lord offers to fund the center, but you refuse out of moral principles and the center has to close. What the fuck, money is money. Every dollar bill out there has been used to buy something harmful during its life, but evil does not stick to the bill (except cocaine I've been told). By refusing to accept "tainted" money, your center no longer helps people and the drug lord was denied a chance to do something good for the community as restitution. Loosen up and accept help that is offered.

Sometimes Divine gifts look like adversity or the last things you would ever want to happen. We all have limited vision and cannot always discern what is best for ourselves and others. You may look back at events and realize that what happened was the best that could have happened for all concerned. Or you may see that what was difficult but bearable for a strong person in an event may have crushed a weaker person, had the weak one received that difficult outcome in the same event. For example, in a terrorist bomb attack, an athlete may have been disabled, but his body may have protected a child who would not otherwise have survived the blast.

Finally, you may not be ready to receive gifts from the Universe. For example, let's say you want most of all to be a monk or nun or minister or whatever. The position is offered, but you say, "What, you are offering the opportunity right now? Oh, not now. I mean someday. Let me know the next time there is an opening." Sometimes the Universe only makes its offer once. You must be ready to accept the opportunity when it is offered or take it even if you are not ready, and then make it work. Never, ever refuse aid because you think the timing is wrong. The Universe knows the right time; you do not.

HOMEWORK:

Find someone in great need. This may be someone in your own family, or someone you see frequently. Find out what they think they need. Usually this is an Ego need and not what they really need. While you help them work with what they think they need, try to determine what they really need, which is almost always the solution to some underlying problem they are not aware of. Use your experience of helping them with their expressed problem as a cover for uncovering and working on their real problem. They can accept help for their version of the problem, but seldom for the real issue, which is why they are still in trouble and cannot find a way out. You cannot tell a person their real problem, which usually has to do with the way they interact with the world around them; in other words their Ego life plan is not working. So you have to be stealthy in working around the way they have to change to have a better life, because their Ego will defend itself against any direct attacks.

You may have to model the new way of being that they need to adapt to. Watch carefully for any assistance the Universe may offer or for messages that you may need to alter your approach. For example, if you are dealing with a dependency issue, you may stumble onto articles on that subject or find a friend who has dealt with that kind of problem. You will either succeed or fail to help the person you select. You will either learn what works, or you will learn how tightly people cling to their problems and fail to see their way out. Experience is one thing that can never be taken away from you, so either way you win.

FURTHER READING:

To explore the concept of Karma further, try *Being Nobody, Going Nowhere* by Ayya Khema.

CHAPTER 6

THE ENEMY WITHIN

"We have met the enemy and they are ourselves."

—ANONYMOUS

The goal of Tantra is transformation from what we are now to our ultimate human potential, or at least a much better version of ourselves that is happier and handles life more effectively. We start out in life as helpless babies, and how we view the world depends on the world we are born into and how effective our parents are. Initially we cannot change our world much. We can cry when something is wrong, and hopefully our parents will fix the problem. Beyond that we have to adapt to whatever the world and our parents offer us.

Infancy is a time of change. Gradually our senses and brains mature, and we develop a mental image of ourselves and the world we are born into. We have physical and emotional needs, and we develop ways to get what we need. Initially it may be crying to be fed and changed and smiling to be touched and held. As we age, our bodies, skills, needs, and strategies to meet our needs become more complex. Language and our interactions with parents and others shape how we view ourselves. Early in our development we become skilled enough in changing our surroundings that we no longer have to adapt to our world. The way we view ourselves then becomes relatively fixed, and the way we get what we need becomes habitual. Once we have a life plan that meets our needs and a self-image that is validated by those around us, we lock-in this life plan and resist change by changing the world rather than ourselves. Problem is, the life plan we were given by our parents and early experience may suck, or the world may have changed so much from that of our childhood that we have great difficulty meeting our needs. Then we need to change.

Western Tantra uses the term Ego for our life plan for interacting with our environment, including our self-image. Ego has our habitual behavior patterns, roles, skills, attitudes, and thoughts. These are the enduring behavior patterns that distinguish each of us from others, also known as our persona or Personality. We mistake Ego for our true nature, so threats to our Ego are mistaken for threats to our life, who we think we are. For better or worse, our life plan has met our needs in the past, so any attack on Ego threatens our plans for meeting our future needs, causing fear. Thus Ego has acquired a life of its own and resists change. However as a mere behavior pattern, Ego *can* change and be overcome, so it is known as the False Self. Because our behavior patterns are often inappropriate for events in our environment, Ego is also known as The Enemy Within each of us. Synonyms for Ego include False Self, Personality, persona, and Role. Overcoming Ego, with its wish to remain the same, is our chief obstacle on the Path to spiritual transformation.

⚔ EGO DANGERS: The Western Tantric Path of Ethics is ethical action in the world. The principal spiritual practice of this Path is Love, unconditional love for everyone and every living thing. The Ego cannot do this kind of love; it can only love what feeds it and adores it. It hates that which threatens its well-being. But the Universe includes everything within it and does not label parts of itself good or bad. Ego often hates Reality, because Reality is always showing Ego its shortcomings. Ego separates the parts of Reality that it likes and calls them "good" and "me," and what it does not like, it calls "bad" and "them." Ego thinks it is God or wants us to serve it as if it were God—to give to Ego everything we have because it deserves it. But to join with God we must give to all others, which means not giving everything to Ego. Ego thinks it will starve, so it will trip up our efforts to reach God, full union with Reality.

Watch out for Ego as you embark on the Path, or the shit will really hit the fan. I once had a friend that I invited to a weekly meditation group that worked on overcoming Ego and developing universal Love. He proclaimed the session he attended wonderful and promised to become a weekly participant. However, the day before the next session he slipped and fell on the one oil spot on the floor of an auto repair shop that was so immaculate that you could eat off the floor. He was injured so badly that he was never able to attend that meditation group again. I believe his Ego subconsciously sabotaged his conscious intent to attend the weekly meditations which were designed to overcome Ego.

Another Ego trick to avoid change includes reading an article or listening to a talk while measuring each statement against a set of Facts the Ego has adopted to define its world view and defend itself against change. When a threat to the Ego or its world view is detected, the Ego slaps the label "wrong!" on the entire article or talk and its source, rejecting everything from that source as fake or lies. This is a favorite tactic for Egos which build their world views from Facts not held by the mainstream. Because we are human and always make a few mistakes, this Ego protection technique works on everything. For example, only one climate research study allegedly faked its results, but this enabled climate change deniers to disregard hundreds of other studies and the agencies that published them. The antidote for this Ego protection trick is changing the "wrong!" label to "maybe wrong, maybe true" and set just that item aside in the part of the brain that keeps things that need to be checked out.

Other favorite Ego protection tactics include becoming too busy or too tired to look for new solutions to problems, forgetting or distorting inconvenient information, altering memory, and losing things. For example, I had a lovely, generous, younger friend with many health problems as a result of diet and exercise habits. Over the years, I gave my friend four books about overcoming Ego and unlocking our inner healing power. My friend managed to lose all four books, despite promises to read them. So I tried reading aloud the *Pain as the Path* section of this book, but my friend fell asleep before I finished. Modeling healthy behavior was equally ineffective, and my dear friend died twenty years my junior.

The Ego will do anything to avoid the risk of destruction, even kill the Body to get away from a life situation that exposes the Ego's limitations. For example, after the 1929 stock market crash, many formerly rich people killed themselves rather than change their self-image from rich to poor. So that is a danger on the Tantric Path to personal transformation: Egos will do *anything* to avoid change.

ALL EGOS REPRESENT SEPARATION from the Divine world, so the most difficult Egos to set aside are those that are very effective dealing with the Material world. Knowing Ego's power, I found a way to befriend my Ego to allow change. First, I moved my self-identity to my Heart center, my Soul. This took time. Then I called Ego what it is, a plan for dealing with my environment, a persona. Next my nameless Soul gave Ego my name in this life, praising it by name for the excellent job it has done in this life with navigating the pitfalls of this world and keeping this Body-Mind-Soul system together and healthy. Then I told Ego that the world we live in will pass away in time, and Ego's only hope for avoiding eventual doom is to help Soul transform and blossom into its immortal essence. My Soul promised to remember this current Ego and whenever it is the best persona for dealing with a situation, then that Ego behavior pattern will be invoked to live again to do what it does best. Conversely, if Ego sabotaged Soul's efforts to evolve, Soul would forever reject this Ego, never to be seen again. The mortal Body's only hope for resurrection to Divine energy was always the Enlightened Soul, so in this way I recruited all parts of my existence, Body, Ego, and Soul, to work together as a team to achieve Tantric transformation. This worked for me. It might work for you.

✳ SELF-LOVE: This might be a good time to mention loving oneself. I think many people love themselves entirely too much, to the exclusion of others. Yet most spiritual writings say it is essential to love oneself before one can love others. What resolves this paradox? The answer lies with a clear understanding of who we are. We are complex creatures and are more physically similar to one another than different. Compare a mass murderer and a saint.

They are about the same physical size and strength; both look human. But one kills people and the other helps people. What is the difference? Many have tried and failed to find inherent physical differences between them, structural differences that require us to be what we are. Ignoring rare abnormalities like missing limbs, the truth is, we are mostly alike. Anything that most humans can do, we can also do. The human body and brain are very adaptable and any of us, given the right conditions, could have become either mass murderers or saints, because we all have the same human potential. Each of us has the capacity to be a killer or a saint or anything in between.

There are some genetic differences that influence who we become, but mostly we were raised to be a particular way, sharing and helping or born to be hanged. We define ourselves in this particular way and match our behavior to this standard, saying things like, "Yes, that's how I roll" or "I'm sorry, that was not like me." We take behaviors that match our internal standard as "me" and those that do not as "not-me," and codify these into our Egos, our plans for interacting with the world. When we see "not-me" behaviors in others we think we would never do that or we are not capable of that. The truth is, most human behavior is well within our capability, or would have been if we had started young and worked at it, or if fortune had favored or cursed us.

So to Love all others, we need to realize that the things we dislike in others are things that we dislike in ourselves, things we assigned to the "not-me" behaviors that we are also capable of, given the right circumstances. The wise are aware of this. In December 2015, when Good Morning America asked Kobe Bryant why some view him as a villain and others see him as a hero, he said we are all both heroes and villains. If we want to avoid doing things that we think are horrible, we need to know that those things are in us.

We are capable of doing horrible things if we fail to watch ourselves closely. To cage our inner beast, we need to know that it is part of who we are, and know it well, so we know when it will try to rule us. To know intimately is to love, so we must love all aspects of ourselves to know and control our inner beast. If we can Love all parts of ourselves, we can Love all others unconditionally.

To own that the beast is part of us is not the same as letting it out, and we can love and pity those who have lost control of theirs. It is a dangerous world, and the beast has a function. People have fought off bears who have attacked them or dragged off loved ones, and won the fight with sheer ferocity. Love your beast, but do not let it rule you. When an enraged parent "loses it" and beats up a child and goes to prison, instead of hating that parent, remember times when you almost lost control of your anger and say with gratitude, "There but for the grace of God go I."

✂ EGO PROTECTION: When you embark on the Western Tantric Path of Ethics, yours is not the only Ego to be concerned about. One of the functions of an Ego, one of the main reasons we have Egos in the first place, is to protect us from harm caused by the Egos of people we come in contact with. Egos separate us from the rest of the world, which is a good thing if we are surrounded by harmful people, which we all are to some degree. People put us down to make themselves feel superior. They feed their own Egos by showing themselves to be better than we are, at our expense. Some people use us to elevate their own importance or to accomplish their own agendas. The same Ego that separates us from the Divine realm and prevents us from reaching our own highest potential is also the Ego that separates us from people who would exploit and harm us. Ego is like an armored shell surrounding our vulnerability.

As you fully commit to helping others, you will encounter people who will take advantage of that and call on you for help often, and it will be for the most menial assistance, such as moving furniture or acting as a sounding board for complaints. You become part of their world. What they are doing is recruiting you into their Ego structure, their plan for dealing with their world. It is important that you do not get sucked into this, because all you are doing is supporting their Ego structure that cannot deal with everyday problems without you. So serving their needs actually hurts them by removing their incentive to change. Rather than harden your own Ego structure that you are trying to soften and change, you have to set strict limits with these people, even relatives. Especially relatives. Tell them what you can do for them and when. Challenge their need for help if you have to, and be sure your help actually helps them rather than makes you a co-dependent. Tantra is a fierce Path, and nothing about it requires that you become a wimp or someone's personal slave.

✄ WORLD EGOS: I do not believe in a satanic evil entity with a plan to lead us to destruction. However we have presented the possibility that the entire universe is conscious, and parts of the Material world seem to try to keep us imprisoned within it to serve and maintain it. My smart phone and computers seem to try to enslave me at times. Certainly the Egos of the people we personally benefit will try to keep us in roles where we serve their needs. So expect push-back from people, and perhaps from aspects of the Material world, if you try to change yourself. Be prepared for the world "dumping on you," and be ready to persist in the face of opposition. If you quit, the Egos win, and you are enslaved.

On the Path of Ethics, you are going to continue to be a responsible steward of your Body and Material support systems. You will continue to pay your bills, keep your job, service your car, do your housework, and all this will distract you from the work of spiritual transformation. However when this happens, go back to your process of change as soon as the distractions let up. It helps to minimize the Material possessions that you have to maintain and to keep your life as simple as possible. By always returning to the Path, the distractors will eventually tire of trying to recruit you and move on to others who are more willing to serve them.

✂ EGO CHANGE: One characteristic of Ego or selfish behavior is trying to create an artificial environment around itself to feel comfortable, safe, or in control. Reality is none of those. Reality is often disturbing or uncomfortable, slightly dangerous, and subject to unexpected change. Ego is our life plan for dealing with our environment, and Ego wants us to think it has everything covered. But we go out into life and shit happens, which causes us to question Ego's life plan. Ego wants us to forget about those moments when its life plan fails. While shit is happening, to protect its plan, Ego finds fault with others and blames all problems on outside forces and other people. It's all the fault of (insert Ego's favorite scapegoat here: bad luck, corporate greed, politicians, liberals, conservatives, taxes, ethnic or religious groups, immigrants, or other outside forces), or it's all the fault of whatever person happens to be nearby when the unwanted event happens.

The last thing Ego wants us to do is question our own life plan, because if our True Self, our Soul, were to stop supporting Ego and expose its limitations and its need to change and adapt, then Ego might lose its control over us and dissolve like the fiction it is. So when shit happens, Ego blames it all on anything but itself. Then Ego takes us to its artificial shell of protection, which could be a home in a nice neighborhood surrounded by people who agree with Ego's life plan. Or Ego's shelter of protection could be an alcohol or drug induced mental state, or comfort in food, music, or physical activity. The new Ego shelters are electronic media, going online. No matter how fucked up we are, we can always find someone who agrees with us online or is worse than we are to validate how okay we are. No matter how bizarre our belief system, Ego can find us comfort with an online community that supports us. With smoke, mirrors, and magic, Ego convinces us that there is no need to change, that despite outside forces, Ego can always get us to a safe place.

But this is a lie. The world is not a safe place; it never has been and never will be. At any moment a plane could crash on us or with us aboard, a natural disaster could strike, a drunk driver could lose control, an illness could strike. The Tantric solution is to embrace change, seek challenge, and find joy in experiencing raw reality.

The next time your life partner criticizes you, try to see that it is their Ego plan conflicting with your Ego plan, and you are both equally to blame. Both of you must change and adapt to get along. If you feel bad about being a salesman for an arms manufacturer, stop blaming the company for making you feel bad about yourself and start training and searching for different work. When you see a drunk passed out in a doorway, instead of looking away, look at him and think, "This is real. He is escaping from a life he does not want with a bottle." Then instead of escaping from a hard day at work by going to your warm home to have a beer, instead at least look at him and maybe do something dangerous like leave him some money or some food or warm clothing. When you buy your next car, instead of picking one that cocoons you in luxury and soft music and insulates you from traffic noise and the road, realize that there is nothing you will be doing that is more dangerous than hurtling your body down a roadway full of potholes at the speed of a cheetah chasing prey, along with a bunch of drivers in two-ton tanks texting or angry or not paying attention. Choose a car with good road feel and visibility that handles and brakes well instead of one with luxury and style. And when you drive it, turn down the stereo and stay sharp. Even Ego will have trouble blaming an accident on the other guy if you are dead.

Wherever you go and whatever you do, experience the world in its raw reality and realize that we are here to experience life and learn from it, not escape from it. That is the Tantric way.

HOMEWORK:

1. Do some journaling. Whenever something happens that upsets you, write down the event and who or what you would *like* to blame for what happened. Be honest. Then cross out the outside person or conditions that you would like to blame, and write down what you could have done or done better to have a better outcome.

2. Do you feel the author is "talking down" to you or repeating instructions as if you are stupid or uneducated? If you answer yes, then three things may be occurring. First, you did not read the author's Preface where he explains why he uses simple words and repetition. Second, you are projecting onto the author your own opinion of why the author is using simple words and repetition, and this is a function of your own Ego. Unless you are clairvoyant, you cannot know the mind and motivation of others, only the reason *you* would have written in that style. Maybe

the author is the one who is stupid and is "talking up" to you using the biggest words he knows. You should reread the start of Chapter 4 and this chapter. Third, if you take Pride in your education and your ability to decipher erudite disquisitions, then you are placing yourself superior to others who lack this skill. If this is the case, you should apply the antidote for Pride found in Chapter 10.

3. On a warm day when it rains, find a nude resort or private location. Instead of wearing rain gear to keep your clothes dry, take off all your clothes. Feel the rain on your body and notice that it is waterproof. And the rain feels nice on your bare skin.

FURTHER READING:

The definitive guide to understanding and transcending Ego is *A New Earth* by Eckhart Tolle. Read this if you need more help overcoming Ego.

CHAPTER 7

TANTRIC TECHNOLOGY

"To see a world in a grain of sand and heaven in a wild flower,
Hold infinity in the palm of your hand
and eternity in an hour."

—WILLIAM BLAKE,

AUGURIES OF INNOCENCE

Tantra uses several key methods to obtain its results. As methods for applying Tantric science and philosophy, these key methods can be considered to be Tantric Technology. In combination, the following methods distinguish Tantra from other spiritual Paths.

 VISUALIZATION: If we want to be better than our selfish Ego, the first thing we should do is decide what sort of person we want to become. What is the result we are looking for? We could do this by choosing the adjectives we want to describe our ideal

version of ourselves. Hopefully it will be words like ethical, trustworthy, loving, compassionate, brave, competent, wise, and other
valued qualities. Pick the best version of a human you can imagine.
Aim high. Ethical atheists can choose heroes and cultural archetypes. Religious people should choose to have the qualities of their
supreme being.

Most religions have concepts of a supreme being. Be careful
of this. Often the concept is of a male figure dispensing perks to
devoted followers and harsh justice to deviants from the faith and
unbelievers, sort of a celestial super-dad. Many of us are repelled
by these visions and have fallen away from established religions
as a result.

If the established religions are correct, we doom ourselves if
we choose wrongly, so each religion asks us to choose their version
of the supreme being, and damns the other versions. But if they are
correct, that we are damned if we choose wrongly, why would we
trust *any* religion's version of ultimate reality? If the religious leaders are wrong, we are the ones who will pay for their mistakes. For
my part, if I am to be doomed, I want it to be for my own mistakes,
not for blindly following someone else.

My Heart says a God worth following will not care about our
religion or race or gender or sexual preference or country or even
species or solar system or our past, only the present quality of our
Souls. A God I could follow and emulate is one that benefits and
loves everyone, cares for the ultimate well-being of both criminals
and their victims, both the oppressed and their oppressors, loving
all and hating none.

So when you try to become the hands of God in the world, be
your own Heart's best version of God in the world. If you have no
concept of a god, then create one that you wish existed, and act in
the world as if your wish were true. If your Heart's wish is true, if

the way you think Ultimate Reality should be is actually the way it is, then the Universe will let you know. And then you will find that vision of Ultimate Reality in all the established religions and philosophies, and signs of that Reality in the sciences. If you get it right, you will.

A word of caution, don't let your Ego create its god—it will just be in Ego's own image and will be a god that benefits itself more than others, a bad parent that has a favorite child. If you find a version of god that treats people worse than you do, destroying whole towns for not worshiping correctly for example, then you have found a god concept created by someone's Ego or a fairy tale to explain natural disasters. To find a true vision of Reality we need to find the part of ourselves that reflects this Reality. To that which is part of all that exists, all parts of Reality are important and no part has a special position, including the part each of us inhabits.

If you act in the world to benefit you alone, that is what your Ego has been doing since you were born. You will learn nothing new from doing what you have always done. To act as the hands of God in the world, you must find your Heart, the part of you that cares about others.

After choosing a working version of your ultimate human who reflects Divine nature in contact with Reality, your next step in Tantric visualization is to see yourself as having already attained that Divine nature, and try to act at all times as if you already have all those qualities. Try to be the hands of God in the world, doing what God would do if God were in your place, or act as if you have already become your ultimate version of a human being. Be what you want to become. If you are persistent in seeing yourself in this way and acting in this way in thought, word, and deed, you will eventually transform into your best version of yourself. In Tantric practice in the irreverent West, we sometimes call this the "fake-it-until-you-make-it" method of personal transformation.

You may find that your concept of the ultimate human or God in the world changes as you evolve. Just adjust your vision and actions as you gain experience. As your concept of Reality begins to match actual Reality, you will notice that what you do works better than before, and your progress with transformation becomes easier and faster. When the student is ready, the teachers appear. Eventually, if your concept of the way the Universe should-be matches the-way-it-is, the sentient Universe should send you signs that you are on the right track. Miracles and magic become visible.

Again be wary of Ego. If you start seeing yourself as superior, you ain't. If you start understanding things that others do not, you are not better; you are luckier. We are all made of the same stuff and have the same ultimate capacity. Eventually everyone will be where you are, in this life or the next. Some of us have had better teachers or are at different stages of spiritual maturity. Especially do not let your Ego tell others you are the hands of God or Jesus or Allah or Buddha or other exalted beings. You may be put on a watch list or a 72-hour psychiatric hold. In the old days, people who said such things were stoned or burned at the stake. Keep your Tantric practices to yourself or to trusted Tantric advisors.

One way to keep from seeing yourself as superior to others when visualizing yourself as an angel, buddha, saint, prophet, or other heroic figure is to also see all others in this way. See the world as Divine, populated by others in their Divine essence. I know this is difficult the way some people behave in this world. To accomplish this feat, reflect on how beautiful this planet appears from space and what a jewel it is among the other planets. Focus on the marvelous works of humans, like the lights of a city at night, and how many people risk their lives to help others after natural disasters. All people have a Divine essence, no matter how deeply buried. Train yourself to see that even in difficult people. When you see yourself surrounded by angels, becoming one yourself will not feed your Ego.

✂ GURUS AND GUIDES: In the Eastern Tantras, finding a trustworthy spiritual advisor, a guru, and doing exactly what the guru says is considered essential. That usually works in the East because the gurus have certifications from where they were taught, sort of like spiritual PhD diplomas. The certifying lineage maintains quality-control functions over its gurus. Although teachers and priests revered by their spiritual traditions do visit the West, in general we are the "wild west" and cannot expect to find anyone we can rely on without question.

With Western Tantra, we listen to teachers who seem to know what they are saying, and read philosophical works that have stood the test of time, but we check out what they say with others, and compare it to our Heart of compassion. Still, the Tantric Path, like most spiritual traditions, is filled with dangers, and we may find ourselves lost in dead-ends or painful states of mind. It would be best if we had someone to confide in. How do we find them, and how do we distinguish between trustworthy advisors and cult leaders?

Just as with finding help for car troubles on the road, it is generally better to look for help yourself rather than wait for someone to approach you. If you are looking for an individual, try established religions, ones that have been around more than one founder's lifetime and have withstood the test of time. The religion you grew up with is a good place to start. Individuals from other sources usually charge for advice.

Personally I prefer groups rather than individuals, and the established religions are good places to look for discussion groups. As with individuals, other sources of groups and clubs usually charge for their time. It is okay to contribute to sustain a group, but paying hourly rates or mandatory large sums for spiritual help could exclude you from help if you are poor.

Prepare to shop around. Tantra is an esoteric and Mystical Path, and people who understand that are hard to find. What should you look for? You usually want people who seem happy with themselves and others. Groups should be open to new members, and they should be as easy to leave as to join. Members should interact with the surrounding community. Their belief system should be published or available to outsiders and free from prejudices and scapegoats.

Warning signs are new groups and those led by one person or a small group of elites, especially if they claim unique knowledge that they are not willing to share freely. There should be little or no hierarchy, because no one holds a special place in the Universe. There should be no fees for guidance or knowledge, only voluntary contributions to sustain the organization or facility. God does not charge for help. The organization should not isolate itself from the surrounding community. We are trying for union with Reality, not separation. Hopefully by following these guidelines you will not find yourself drinking poison so that your spirit can join aliens on a spacecraft bound for paradise.

✂ OPENING THE HEART: If we persistently help others, we will become proficient at detecting suffering in others. At first we may simply notice another's body language. Eventually we will open up to others and really empathize with their pain. Initially we may think, "I have enough pain of my own. I don't need to feel the suffering of others!" But if we let our Heart open, we find that empathizing with others actually feels good. It feels like connecting with the world, a sort of better Internet. By comparison, the way we were before felt isolated and numb. Feeling the hurt of others is bittersweet, and it feels good to touch Reality in this way. We feel more alive. As the Universe feels for its creatures, we too feel for them. Our Soul, our Divine center, opens to the rest of Reality. We begin to feel for others what God must feel.

I was once walking toward a school when I saw a man with no arms. I thought he might have lost them to a disease like diabetes. My nose itched, and I suddenly realized he could not scratch his nose. My heart opened to him for a moment, and I burst into tears, thinking if there were a way to do it, I would give him one of my arms. The feeling only lasted a moment, as reason stepped in and said: if poor circulation was the cause, then he would just lose the arm again. But for that moment, I really felt for the man, and knew I had a Heart that worked. To know your Heart works, that is really something.

✂ PATIENCE: The Western Tantric Path of Ethics leads us to consistently perform acts of kindness for others that are not intended to benefit ourselves. As we do these acts resembling unconditional Love, eventually someone's story will touch us, and our Heart opens and connects with Reality. We feel Love and become Love. The sentient Universe notices this flare of Light in the Dark, and helps us transform. Magic becomes real for us, and progress becomes faster.

Until we connect with Reality, a problem with any spiritual Path is this: we do the work, but nothing seems to happen. Patience is what sustains us when nothing is happening. The problem is like screwing a light bulb into a socket. We turn the bulb, but nothing happens. If we persist, the end of the bulb eventually contacts the source of power in the depth of the socket, and suddenly the bulb lights. The spiritual Path is like that; eventually our consciousness grows deep enough to reach our Heart center, which holds Divine power, and our consciousness suddenly lights up. We become part of Divine consciousness, accessing the power of the Universe that flows through us. So have Patience and keep working.

✂ COMMITMENT: A foundation of Eastern Tantric tradition is initiation, which is basically a promise to persist with practice for a lifetime. Initiation is usually an elaborate ceremony designed to impress the practitioner with the gravity of the lifetime commitment to continue the practice. Western Tantra has no commitment ceremonies, but Commitment to persist with the practices for a lifetime is no less important. Western Tantra is not trying to create a new religion, because there is nothing fundamentally wrong with the religions and philosophies that we already have. Certainly there are serious problems with the way people interpret the writings of our spiritual traditions and the way they follow or fail to follow the lessons, but the wisdom behind the established religions is sound. Accounts from all the well-established religions and philosophies describe followers who have had high realizations of Ultimate Reality and have passed into the life beyond. There are even more numerous accounts from people who claim these Divine beings manifest in various ways to assist us in life and with our transition to the next life. We call these Divine guides for their Paths angels, buddhas, and other terms. Most of us only see their effects in the world, but many have seen manifestations. If you do not believe this, ask around with an open mind. Better yet, open your Heart and see for yourself.

Western Tantra is a new version of an ancient Path and has no Divine guides yet, because as of this writing, no one practicing Western Tantra has passed to the life beyond this one. So the way to commit to a lifetime of practice in Western Tantra is to take your Commitment through the religion or philosophy you currently have, or choose an established religion or philosophy if you have none. This could be in the form of baptism, confirmation, mitz-vah, declaration, refuge, initiation, vows, promises, or a host of other forms of commitment. Think of this as signing up for assistance from those of your tradition who have gone before. We will call the religion to which you commit, your Base religion or philosophy.

Personally I have a dual religious practice. I kept my Episcopal Christian foundation when I adopted Tibetan Tantric Buddhism, and as I progressed in Buddhism from refuge to lay vows and highest Tantric initiations, I balanced these new commitments by renewing my Episcopal confirmation and continuing Christian and other religious study. Properly understood at the Mystical level, I find no conflict among any of the religions, or with West-ern science for that matter. Mystics of all the religions and top scientists seem to have no problems understanding one another. It is the literalists and fundamentalists who seem to think their way is the only way.

I should note that if you choose more than one tradition for your commitments, do not pick and choose concepts to make up your own belief system cafeteria-style. Each tradition is more or less internally consistent, at least at the esoteric and Mystical level. Each has concepts which may seem obscure or wrong until you understand them in depth. If you just pick the parts you like, that is Ego doing the choosing. You have to keep each religion and philosophy whole and intact, or they probably will not work.

Here is an analogy. Let's say you are building a hotrod out of a Corvette and a Ferrari. You cannot take the parts you like out of the American V8 and the Italian V12 engines to make one engine. The parts are not designed to work together. However, you *could* put both the complete V8 and the complete V12 into one twin-engine hotrod and have both engines power that very fast car. By keeping both my Christian and Buddhist practices complete, I find I am having experiences from both traditions, and each helps explain the other. This is called a "dual practice." I like to think I have both angels and buddhas helping me along my Path.

Wherever you take your Commitments, please add at least one Commitment to never take your own life. Refusing life-extending medical procedures does not count as taking your own life. As you will see when we discuss adversity, we can encounter great difficulty on any journey through life. Adversity makes us stronger, and the Universe may have plans for us that require more strength than other humans may need. We do not know our ultimate potential; only the sentient Universe knows our highest purpose. Our Ego may hate our current life and may wish to terminate our current life to escape from the lessons this life is trying to teach. To prevent losing the future the Universe is preparing us for, please make an additional commitment to never commit suicide. God knows when it is our best time to leave this life; we do not.

SECRET PRACTICE: When we discover something wonderful, most of us wish to share it with others. We brag or evangelize. In Tantra it is considered better to keep your spiritual realizations to yourself. There are several reasons for this. If you describe your progress to anyone with an Ego, and that is almost everyone, then their Ego will try to show that their experiences are better or that yours are worse. This can undermine your confidence in your experiences and strengthen the Egos involved in this encounter, both yours and those of the other people involved.

Also, most spiritual experiences are indescribable, because language was designed to interact with the Material world, not the Divine. We have no words to describe the ineffable, no pictures to show the invisible, and no forms to give shape to the Formless. All expression falls short.

In the unlikely event that you do find words to capture the experience, you may create expectations that will hinder those you tell, because their contact with the Divine may take different forms, depending on their unique inner worlds. We all experience life differently and are on different parts of the Path. Some may think you are nuts.

But mostly you should keep spiritual experiences to yourself to keep others from stomping on your dream. An analogy will illustrate this. If you still have an Ego, the Ego or False Self surrounds and protects you from the outside world, the way a shell protects a seed. The shell protects us, but it also keeps us from breaking out to become our True Nature until we are ready. We think our True Nature is the hard shell, but it is actually the plant inside that it will become. When the seed falls on good earth, if it first sends out a leaf, something will eat it and the plant will not grow. That is like revealing your spiritual experiences before they are strong. However, if the seed first sends out roots hidden in the good soil before sending up leaves, then if something eats the leaves, more will grow from the roots. This is how Tantric practitioners should approach their practice. Break out of your shell in secret, put down strong roots in solitude and perhaps with trusted spiritual advisors in private, then show your True Nature when you are strong enough to resist those who would bring you down.

How do you identify advisors you can trust? Tell them something small, and see how they react to that. Do not reveal core issues until advisors have proven themselves helpful. This flushes out false gurus who will tear you down in order to rebuild you in their own image, or use you for their own plans and dreams.

HOMEWORK:

1. Pick a hero or Divine figure to emulate. List the qualities of this figure that you want to acquire. Keep a journal of your progress, where you succeed and where you fail and why.

2. Try to locate a person or group you can trust to confide in to help overcome problems.

3. Find a spiritual tradition or philosophy you are willing to commit to, which we will call your Base religion or philosophy. Make a formal commitment to follow the principles of that religion or philosophy. Be sure to include a commitment not to commit suicide.

   If you want to identify yourself as a Western Tantric practitioner (which technically is an Ego self-identification, but possibly beneficial as a step on the Path to change), use it as an adjective for your Base religion or philosophy. Call yourself a Western Tantric [insert the names for your Base religion, philosophy, or practice here]. For example, I call myself a Western Tantric Episcopal Buddhist.

   If you call yourself Western Tantric, never think your way is the only way. The last thing we need on Earth is another religious Path that calls all the other religions wrong and worthy of violent destruction. If you label yourself with the Western Tantric brand, it means that you subscribe to the belief that all time-tested spiritual Paths lead to the same result, and apparent differences are merely different approaches that use different terms to refer to the same thing. For example, the Universal Christ existed from the beginning of time (John 1:1) and is found in all valid Paths, regardless of how this is expressed using our flawed language skills. So the statement that there is no way to the Father but through Christ (John 14:6) refers to the Universal Christ present in all valid Paths. Allah is the same Totality that includes everything that exists, has existed, or ever could exist, so by definition there is only one, there can be no other God, and we see this same God in all religions and philosophies regardless of how the concept is labelled.

Western Tantric practitioners know that all human concepts of the world, including religions, are part of the life plans of the Ego, which is an imaginary concept with no physical reality and can change as a human matures. Therefore, it is an error to think that a scriptural instruction to destroy wrong believers means to kill physical human Bodies. The believer is the Ego, not the Body or the Soul. The Western Tantric practitioner may decide to attack and destroy harmful Ego beliefs using the sword of Truth wielded with wisdom, but tries never to destroy or damage physical human Bodies. Human Bodies are precious gifts from the Universe used to house Divine Souls. All Divine Souls will eventually find their ultimate existence, regardless of their Path, and may switch Paths, blurring the distinction between religions. If you call yourself Western Tantric, do not interpret the scriptures of your Base religion or philosophy literally with your Ego; instead use your Heart of Love and compassion.

FURTHER READING:

One of the best explanations of Tantra from a Tibetan High
Lama considered by many of his followers (including me) to be
Enlightened is *Introduction to Tantra: A Vision of Totality* by Lama
Thubten Yeshe.

CHAPTER 8

TANTRIC MEDITATIONS

"Do every act of your life as though
it were the very last act of your life."
—MARCUS AURELIUS, *MEDITATIONS*

R ather than focus on meditation, on the Western Tantric Path of
Ethics we are mostly performing acts of Love in the Real world.
But there are some types of meditation which can help develop the
mental states needed to be able to do this well.

✵ MINDFULNESS: In Tantra, we are trying to put everything
we have into transforming our life from ordinary to transcendent.
So unlike our regular jobs or temporary roles, we want to practice
all our waking hours. This is actually possible using a technique
called Mindfulness, which means paying full attention to whatever you are doing at all times. Other ways of saying this are to
"live in the moment" or "be present." Mindfulness is a type of

meditation and the principal practice of Zen. When you walk, walk. When you clean house, clean house.

Our typical mode of being in the West is multitasking. So in the West, while cleaning house or walking or doing other simple tasks, we typically plan for the future and review what we did in the past. Thinking this way, we are not paying full attention to what we are doing, and we make mistakes, which cause us to have to think about how to do better in the future. Distracted from the present moment, we make even more mistakes, and we have to think about those.

But the past cannot be changed and the future does not yet exist and may unfold differently than we plan, rendering all that thought a waste of time. Imagine how much more efficient it would be to pay attention to what we are doing in order to reduce the chance of missteps that we have to regret, and then re-plan for the future. Using Mindfulness to avoid mistakes saves a lot of time and puts us in the present moment, which is the only moment in time when we can actually change what is happening or about to happen.

We prefer reacting to things that happened rather than acting in the moment, because paying attention takes more mental effort. But try being in the moment, and you may find that performing better saves time and gives you more spare time to relax. Then when you relax, relax. When you go to sleep, sleep. Maybe sleep will be easier if there are no mistakes to rehash and regret.

I have always complained to the Universe about not having enough time to meditate, so I tried Mindfulness meditation while driving, because driving was the only peaceful spare time I had available. Basically this means paying complete attention to driving, allowing no distracting thoughts. Concentrating on driving was more work mentally, but eventually driving became more fun, because when I could see how the other drivers were interacting with the road and traffic; I could see what they needed to do and see subtle clues revealing what they would do next. It almost felt like reading their minds, and I could tell when to fall back, speed up, or change lanes to help them do what they needed to do to avoid crises. Driving became smoother and more fun when I could really see what was happening and "go with the flow."

When I told friends that I meditated while driving, they were horrified, thinking I closed my eyes and tuned out the outside world. The truth was the opposite. By paying full attention to the task at hand and acting rather than reacting, I became better at the task and still had the inner peace that meditation brings. Instead of trying to find time for meditation, try Mindfulness meditation, focusing intently on whatever you need to do, and see what happens.

MINDFULNESS IS NOT JUST FOR MEDITATION, it can also keep us alive. Life is hazardous, and if we are not paying close attention to what we are doing, we may make fatal mistakes or fail to see hidden dangers. Using the above example of driving a car, about three thousand people die in auto accidents each month in the United States. That death toll is almost equal to one 9/11 World Trade Center catastrophe every month. If you want to know one of the main areas where Darwinian selection is taking place, it is on our roads. Think about that the next time you want to multitask while driving.

Work environments can also be hazardous. In my health and safety profession, I have investigated many accidents that resulted from inattention. I have seen disabling injuries caused by stepping off a curb wrong or slipping on a stack of magazines. A beloved fireman was killed walking into a downed high voltage power line. It pays to pay attention at work.

Robberies, construction zone accidents, weather emergencies, animal attacks, and active-shooter incidents are rarer than highway and work incidents, but in these cases the victims often walk into the danger without noticing until it is too late. Mindfulness would help.

The safety we typically feel is an illusion. We cannot even walk around our homes safely without paying attention. A moment's inattention is all it takes to slip in the tub or shower, step on a round toy on the stairs, slip on the ice out front, fall off the roof or a ladder, or fail to see a host of other household hazards. Most accidents happen in the home. Stay vigilant.

As a spiritual technique, Mindfulness, paying full attention to what we are doing while we are doing it, has a very special effect. It makes us present in the moment. We then live life while we are living it. Our Heart-Mind catches up to the present moment and we experience Reality. We experience our lives as God experiences life, and our Souls open up to the Universe. We begin to awaken.

✖ REFLECTION: On some regular schedule you should go somewhere quiet to experience solitude and silence, so that you can think clearly. This is Reflection. Most people dislike this because negative thoughts and emotions often arise when we are quiet. If we stay busy, we suppress the thoughts of what is wrong with our lives and ourselves. So the question is, do you want to face these doubts now when you are strong and healthy, or later when you are forced to be quiet and alone as you are sick or dying?

We need to practice Reflection when things are okay, so we can rid ourselves of crippling doubts and fears while we are strong and our minds are clear. As immortal Souls experiencing life on one of the most beautiful planets in the universe, at one of the most interesting times in history, in a Western country that is free and prosperous, we should be experiencing joy. If we are not, we have problems with our Egos, our expectations and plans for relating to our environments.

Most if not all of the fears and sufferings we experience come from our Egos. Our Egos may not be experiencing the lives they want and expect and feel they deserve. Or changes in the world may require Ego to change, in essence become a different person to deal with the new reality. The Ego fears change as a type of annihilation. Surrender to the moment that is now, and accept change gracefully. To feel better, become better.

Let negative thoughts and emotions bubble up during quiet Reflection in a safe place free from distractions. Exposed to the bright light of Reality, you may see that these negative thoughts are mostly illusions. The past cannot be changed so there is no point worrying about that. The future does not yet exist, so as soon as you have done what you can in the present, there is no point in experiencing future problems until they arrive, if they arrive at all. Focus on how things are now and do the best you can do now. I often find that while the future looks terrifying, the present moment is very pleasant. I am reminded of the old joke about the guy who falls from the top of a fifty-story building. A window washer on the twentieth floor hears him say as he flashes by, "So far, so good!"

But mostly just let the fears and suffering come out to wash over you and dissipate. You are stronger than your fears. Eventually all the negativities will appear, persist for a time, and then vanish. What remains will be your True Nature as a child of God in a universe so vast that its wonders defy description.

HOMEWORK:

1. The next time you perform a hobby that requires full concentration, notice how focusing on a task in the present moment

interrupts the flow of negative thinking and lets you relax. Try the same focus of attention on a household chore and observe that full attention to that chore has the same effect. Mindfulness creates mental peace, whether the task is something fun or something you would rather avoid.

2. To get a feel for the percentage of people who pay attention to the world around them, try this. While walking outside on a sidewalk or in a park, put away your cellphone and earbuds and count the number of people that could be shot by a domestic terrorist without them noticing, if there were a domestic terrorist with a gun. Don't count out loud. Don't point with a finger or say, "bang." Don't write about that in your journal or post it on social media.

3. See if your busy schedule allows you to have absolute peace and quiet for an hour one day a week, at a set day and time each week. If you have a life partner, coordinate that schedule with your partner, with your partner handling issues that come up during your quiet hour and allowing your partner the same benefit (or a different activity) at another time. Use that hour for Reflection. Shit will happen to take away that hour, and if it does, make your world give you two hours to compensate. If that is taken away, take four hours, and so on. If your life partner is the problem, work it out or start looking for a new life partner.

FURTHER READING:

The best guide to Mindfulness for Westerners is *The Power of Now* by Eckhart Tolle. Where the book *Western Tantra* devotes part of a chapter to being present in the moment, Eckhart Tolle devotes an entire book, with exercises and examples. With each new reading, you will gain fresh insight. Highly recommended.

Also try Thich Nhat Hanh, *The Miracle of Mindfulness*, a beautiful and readable guide to the art of Thien Zen Mindfulness, with universal application for all spiritual traditions. Thich Nhat Hanh is a Vietnamese monk with many books on meditation, inter-being, interfaith, and world peace that are compatible with Western thought.

CHAPTER 9

TANTRIC SEX

*"For Buddhists, sexual intercourse can be used in the spiritual
path because it causes a strong focusing on consciousness
if the practitioner has firm compassion and wisdom."*

—HIS HOLINESS THE 14TH DALAI LAMA, *HOW TO PRACTICE*

N ow we get to the part of this book that all of you have been
waiting for. If you skipped ahead to reach this chapter, go
back to where you left off and read all the chapters. They provide
the foundation needed to understand Tantric sex, which is a very
special form of Mindfulness meditation. Mindfulness and the concepts leading up to it are essential for understanding and making
this practice work. If you are a monk, nun, or priest who has taken
celibacy vows, you may have to skip this chapter entirely because it
is very graphic. *The Red Path of Meditation* will have practices you
can use without breaking vows. If you bought this book just to take
this part out of context to condemn the book, instead just throw
the book in the trash, so that some homeless person who cannot
afford to buy it may find it and benefit from it.

Sex has many methods and meanings in Western culture; let's look at the different types, so that we know what Tantric sex is not.

Plan A: This is sex for personal pleasure, also known as "Lust," one of the more popular forms of sex, especially for the selfish Ego. It can be good for the physical Body, keeping all the sex organs healthy, and can tone the rest of the Body. But as selfish pleasure, it strengthens Ego, and when exploitive it is not ethical; so this is definitely not the sex we are looking for here.

Plan B: Think "B" for babies. This sex is for propagation of the species, a worthwhile function if not carried too far. Survival of the species is best served if males stay horny and females are unsatisfied. Thousands of years of evolution have resulted in women who are hard to bring to orgasm so that they remain unsatisfied and sexually receptive, and men who get off in a few seconds and in a few minutes are ready to go again. Most established religions advocate this approach to create new members, and they require parents to indoctrinate children in their dogma while they are young and easily trained, thus expanding that religion. This goes hand-in-hand with religions acting as the cheerleaders for war against territory occupied by other religions or sects, expanding their religion at the expense of other religions and cultures. Maintaining a healthy population of humans is a noble enterprise, but expanding the world population beyond what the Earth can support, so that all life on Earth is miserable and threatened with extinction, is both stupid and unethical. For these reasons, this form of sex is not part of the Path of Ethics.

Plan C: Think "C" for civilized. The modern form of sex in Western culture is to produce pleasure for both partners as equally as possible, using techniques to achieve simultaneous orgasm. This plan uses birth control, so we do not fill the world with people who will consume the world's resources, driving up prices and ruining parents' credit ratings, which in turn keeps parents from buying stuff for themselves. This is a much more ethical version of Plan A, but it still serves the Egos of the partners and focuses on the Material life; so this is still not the sex we are looking for. Also there are already tons of books on the subject of having satisfying sex. The world does not need another one.

Plan D: Think "D" for Don't. This is celibacy, where people have no sex at all and drive themselves so crazy that there are two possible outcomes. One outcome is becoming so overcome by Lust that they revert periodically to Plan A. A variation on "beer goggles," after a long stint with celibacy, even children and animals start to look desirable. A better outcome for those with strong will is they drive themselves so close to crazy that they have visions of God or other spirit beings, experiencing realms beyond the Material world. This is a form of asceticism required by several legitimate and effective religious Paths. If you are up for this and have the determination to avoid the Plan A pitfall, go for it. But this is not Tantric sex.

Plan E: Think "E" for Ecstasy. Ecstasy is a transcendent state of being in which the False Self or Ego and the entire Material world disappear momentarily, and the discursive mind shuts up, as we dwell in the pleasure of the moment. A special form of Mindfulness meditation, this is exactly the kind of sex we are looking for to accelerate our progress on the Path. In Tantra we use everything we have, including strong emotions, to drive spiritual progress. Sex generates some of our strongest feelings, which can be used to power our practice, transforming sexual energy into the Path of liberation from suffering. Eventually we experience intimate contact with Reality, the well of creation, union with God consciousness. This *is* Tantric sex.

✂ SAFETY TIPS: Sex is not safe. When you have sex with another person, you are playing with fire, Inner Fire. Ironically, my last job title before retirement as a safety professional was Fire Protection Manager, so I am motivated to give you some safety tips to reduce your chance of getting burned.

The first safety tip is to keep your actions ethical. Tantra is not your license to throw out the laws and customs of your human community. Your partner must be of legal age, completely free of psychoactive drugs of any kind, mentally competent, must understand the planned activity, and must agree to participate without any physical, chemical, or psychological coercion whatsoever. You cannot go into a bar and say, "Hey baby, let's do Tantra!" and expect to have anything but the lowest, animal form of sex.

Second, you have to protect yourself and your partner from sexually transmitted diseases, by either using protection or knowing your partner's sexual history. Teachers at a local Zen center incorrectly believed that if they had not generated the Karma to experience disease, they would be immune. Virtue is no protection against tragedy, as you can see by watching the news.

Third, Tantric sex takes time and practice, and caring for an infant takes even more time and prevents other activities, so fertile heterosexual partners should not try to do both at the same time. Use contraception if you do not want to give up Tantric sex in nine months.

Safety tip four: Tantric sex probably works best in a long-term, committed relationship where both partners feel safe, and there is not the distraction of getting to know a new person. Again, Tantric practices often take time and practice to work properly, so if you are not married, pick someone you enjoy spending time with. You must like your partner's feel and smell. If you will not enjoy long periods of naked embrace in intimate genital contact, find a different long-term partner and agree to some sort of committed monogamous relationship.

Safety tip five: As with any meditation technique, if it feels good keep doing it. But if it feels bad, stop and do something else for a while before trying it again. It is possible that Tantric sex may never work for you. If so, try some of the other Western Tantric techniques. This *White Path of Ethics* has an entire body of practices, not just sex. Other Western Tantric Paths may work better for you, such as those found in *The Red Path of Meditation* or *The Blue Path of Union*. Eastern Tantra may be best for you. Perhaps no form of Tantra is right for you, and other religious techniques like devotion and prayer may serve you better. Do not feel bad about yourself; just keep looking for something that works for you.

✂ FUNDAMENTALS OF TANTRIC SEX: This *Western Tantra* book avoids most of the complexity of other texts on the subject. I believe in the engineering mantra, KISS: "Keep it Simple, Stupid!" If you like intricate breathing and complex visualization techniques, go ahead; knock yourself out and use different texts and teachers. No one technique is right for everyone, and you need to find what works for you. What you will find here is Tantric sex boiled down to its essential core without many cultural trappings.

The first principle is for both partners to realize we are trying to find our Soul, which is our Heart center connected to Reality experiencing pure unselfish Love. Soul wants to give pleasure, whereas Ego wants pleasure for itself. So if you want to unlock your Soul, you must suppress all selfish wishes, and focus on giving pleasure to your partner. It is your partner's job to give you pleasure, but you must not think or speak about that during sex, or this will just turn into Plan A, simple Lust. Just concentrate on sending loving energy to your partner.

The second principle is to be open and receptive to whatever pleasurable feelings you may receive, even if they seem overwhelming. Only Ego has limits on how much pleasure or pain it can stand, so set it aside and let your Soul be free to take and give what it will.

The third principle of Tantric sex is for both partners to memorize the steps, so that you do not have to think, talk about, or label what either of you are doing or feeling. Thinking, talking, and labeling are functions of the Material Body and its brain, the discursive mind. You are trying to experience the formless Soul, which is not part of the Material world. The Soul does not use words to sort and classify things. Its thought is intuition, and its language is silent being. Be still and try not to think or generate thoughts. Just focus on any pleasant feelings without labeling them. Just be.

The fourth principle is to make the experience last as long as possible. This is not the passionate, urgent sex of most Hollywood movies, but more like the extended coupling of the two lovers in the film *Dangerous Beauty*. Remembering the types of sex presented earlier, this is not Plan B. Males must retain semen. We are not using sex to procreate, which is best served by exchanging fluids as soon as possible. We are trying to gently awaken something that may have been asleep a long time, our Soul, which generally awakens only when the Body sleeps or is silent.

The fifth principle is that we are actually trying for a spiritual experience, so your physical Body's sexual responses are optional, although very helpful. That may sound odd, so let's discuss the anatomy of the Spirit Body.

✖ SPIRIT BODY: According to the spiritual literature, the Spirit Body or "diamond" body, which inhabits the physical Body, has a hollow central channel from the top of the head to the floor of the pelvis. This central channel is flanked by two thinner channels, said to convey male and female Energy to an Energy center at the navel, where male and female Energy combine to power the Spirit Body. It is sort of like matter and antimatter combining at the dilithium crystal to power a starship, although nothing we are describing is made of ordinary matter or energy. Spirit Energy is distributed within the Spirit Body through the central channel to Energy centers called *chakras* located on the central channel at the crown of the head, the neck, near the heart, near the navel, and near the genitals. Radiating from the chakras are secondary Energy channels called *nadi*, which branch out smaller and smaller to reach all parts of the physical Body, like capillaries that nourish the physical Body. The heart chakra is thought to be the principal location of our Divine center, the seat of consciousness. My spiritual tradition works mainly with five chakras. Other spiritual systems locate more chakras, some outside the Body.

I do not know if this Spirit Body is an actual manifestation of something real or just a convenient way to visualize the Spirit Body in order to control it, the way the human brain projects representations of the physical Body onto the cortex of the brain. Whether real or not, this visualized anatomy of the Spirit Body has been useful for many of us to promote our spiritual well-being. For example, for new Souls, the channels are visualized as being knotted or kinked to prevent Energy flow until the Soul is mature enough to handle the Energy effectively. The physical forms of yoga are thought to open the channels to allow Energy flow. Having led prior lives, some old Souls are thought to have open channels from birth, allowing people like Jesus to do things others cannot.

People who are completely masculine or feminine are thought to have an Energy imbalance that prevents effective spiritual progress, like a bird trying to fly with only one wing. Techniques have been developed in schools of yoga to balance male and female Energy, leading to a more effective human being. Yoga classes can enhance Tantric sex.

I like to think of male and female Energy as the male knowledge of how to do things (skill) and the female knowledge of what to do (wisdom). To be complete human beings, we must combine the female wisdom of what to do with the male knowledge of how to do it if we are to be effective.

Again, I do not know how much this visualization of Spirit anatomy has to do with what is really going on, but the reason to bring it up now is to explain how it relates to our experiences during Tantric sex. First, realize that a Soul in balance has both male and female elements, so in a spiritual sense, physical gender is irrelevant. Souls are essentially androgynous, having both male and female elements, the ability to both penetrate and receive sexual Energy. This you may be able to feel and verify for yourself.

During Tantric sex, both partners may feel sexual penetration. If both partners are pushing sexual Energy into their partners, each receiving partner may feel the penetration all the way from their genitals, up through the central channel, and through the throat chakra. If both partners are capable of doing this deep penetration, it is called Interpenetration, and the intensity of the resulting sexual pleasure can be roughly proportional to the depth of the penetration, far greater than ordinary orgasm. A nice side benefit for males is that this ability to penetrate more than twenty-four inches into your partner has nothing to do with physical penis length.

✂ **THE PRACTICE**: Now that you both have memorized the above principles and the anatomy of the Spirit Body, you are ready to begin. You need to find a time and quiet place where you will not be interrupted for a few hours. Take care of any bodily needs, such as hunger and elimination that could distract or interrupt the practice. Visualize yourself and your partner as Divine beings in a heavenly setting. Removing all clothing is best, so that you may contact your partner as completely and closely as physically possible. However, some Eastern Tantric couples dress themselves as Tantric deities, so such elaborations are okay if this helps visualize yourselves as Divine beings.

Although any sexual position should work, Souls are neither superior nor inferior to one another, and bearing weight can be distracting; so face-to-face in a sitting position probably works best. Most Westerners cannot sit in a lotus position for more than a few minutes, so find a comfortable seat where the two of you can sit facing one another, with the legs of one wrapped around the hips and waist of the other, the way one sees the sexual embrace in Buddhist *thanka* paintings. Try to work out a comfortable sexual position before starting foreplay.

Both partners should use Mindfulness meditation to attain peaceful states of mind and sharp focus on the present activity. Visualize yourselves as Divine beings, and view your acts of Love and your surroundings as sacred.

Use foreplay to arouse each other in the usual way. Ideally the penis or clitoris will be erect and natural lubrication will be flowing for both of you. If one or both of you are dry, you may add lubricating oils or gels. Once well lubricated, for heterosexual couples, the man inserts his penis into the woman's vagina as deeply as possible. Same-sex partners should get their genitals as close together as possible. The couple should move their genitals together slowly and gradually until nearly at the point of conventional orgasm, then stay as near the point of orgasm for as long as possible without male ejaculation, thrusting and stopping as needed to stay at that level. The partners may have to communicate to stay near their peaks, asking for more or less movement, but do not talk of comfort or anything but what you are doing.

Remember that all your intention must be on providing pleasure to your partner, and be open to whatever happens from your side. Initial focus of attention should be on the pleasure of your genitals, and concentrate your sexual Energy there. As pleasure builds, both partners should visualize sexual Energy flowing from their genitals into their partner's genitals and sexual Energy flowing into themselves from their partners. As the embrace continues, imagine a circuit or fountain where you flow Love Energy into your partner through their genitals and up their central channel and Love Energy flows back from your partner to your genitals and up your central channel and through your whole body, mingling their Energy with yours and flowing back into your partner. Continue this visualized Love Energy exchange as long as possible.

Most likely, nothing transcendent will happen, and this will be just a long, pleasant erotic exercise in Mindfulness meditation for both of you. The advantage of sex meditation is that it is much more fun than mindfully sweeping the floor, walking, or doing the laundry. The inherent pleasure and fun of sex helps maintain your focus of attention on the present moment. Repeat these Tantric sex sessions at least weekly. You might think nothing special is happening during these sessions, but you would be wrong. Extended pleasure invites the Soul to awaken. Like the lotus flower growing toward the light until it breaks free of the surface of the water and blossoms, the growing Soul never "un-grows." Beneath the surface of your consciousness, something is happening. Continue these sessions.

At some point during one of your Tantric sex sessions, you may feel a building pleasure, like orgasm, but coursing through your whole Body and far more intense. Just let ecstasy build without stopping it, as much and as long as you can stand the overwhelming pleasure, until it abates or you have to stop to maintain your sanity. Or your partner may experience this, eventually having to stop out of mental exhaustion. If either of you experience this, you are done for the day. The partner who experiences this will need to rest for a few days before trying this again.

Some call this the legendary extended massive orgasm and it can last for many minutes or perhaps even a few hours, even for men as a whole body experience without ejaculating. Few realize the true nature of this experience. This ecstasy is the Soul waking up and is a taste of the life beyond this one and union with the Divine. It brings profound changes. Gradually you will feel as if you are waking up from a dream in which ordinary reality is the dream, and a new reality which seems somehow brighter is your new reality. Love blossoms in the Heart and courage grows as visions of a better life beyond the mundane Material life become real.

✂ HELPFUL TIPS: Here are some Tantric sex tips that may enhance the experience and overcome common problems.

Tip 1: If during or after one of these Tantric sex sessions, you have a vision of a field of clear white light, stay and rest in this vision of clear light as long as possible. The clear light may appear to be a mix of all colors, which combine to appear white. If a small object appears in this clear light, rest your attention on the object as long as possible and see what happens, even if this feels strange to you. Memorize this instruction before starting Tantric sex meditation or any other spiritual practice, so that if this clear light vision appears, you will know what to do without having to stop what you are doing to investigate or wonder what to do. Remaining in the clear light vision as long as possible develops mental stability and is very beneficial.

Tip 2: Notice that at the point near orgasm, you forget your Self, your persona, your Ego. For a moment you are not a lone, separate individual, but instead become one with your partner and your surroundings; you synchronize your movements with your partner's movements as ecstasy builds. This moment of experiencing oneness with Reality provides evidence that the Soul is part of all-that-exists, a taste of Totality.

Tip 3: Staying close to orgasm without ejaculating is difficult for males who orgasm more easily than women do. Erectile assisting drugs like sildenafil can help maintain a stiff erection without coming too close to ejaculation.

Tip 4: After a long session of Tantric sex without coming to full orgasm, male partners will have to switch to conventional sex or masturbation and ejaculate to avoid the painful testicle swelling known as "lover's nuts."

Tip 5: Young men can ejaculate at the mere sight or first touch of a woman. If this prevents sustained sex, wear a condom and reduce movement. If this is not enough for stamina, then before a session, masturbate until the point of orgasm, and then stop stroking and just let the semen flow out without forceful ejaculation until semen stops flowing. Your erection will remain rock hard, and you will be able to keep it up for hours. This method may take some practice. This does not work for older men who are done after ejaculating once.

Tip 6: Do not be discouraged if you or your partner have disabilities that prevent physical sexual intercourse. What we are trying to achieve here is the Interpenetration of Souls. Just as the Soul has its own sensory apparatus, it also has its own sexual Energy and the sexual structures to use it. It may only be necessary to be in close physical contact with your partner to achieve sexual union of Souls. So do not let disabilities of the Body stop you. Your Soul is probably intact and healthy, and it can achieve the same results described above.

Tip 7: If you have no partner at all, try the Tantric sex technique during masturbation. Rather than try for Interpenetration, instead just awaken the sexual Energy and light up the sexual structures of your own Soul. To do this, you want to achieve near-peak maximum sexual pleasure just short of orgasm for as long as possible. Whole-body ecstasy is possible even with solo practice. This is probably easier for a woman than a man, because when a man ejaculates, the fun is over. So as with partner sex, males must stimulate themselves nearly to the point of orgasm but not beyond. This may take practice, but it is fun practice. For both men and women, once at the point of maximum sustained pleasure, remain at that point as long as possible, and be open to a dramatic increase in pleasure. If it happens, do not pull back but instead let ecstasy wash over you. This is the same awakening of the Soul that we described for partner sex; just not quite as fun as sharing.

HOMEWORK:

1. Memorize the Tantric sex principles and Spirit Body anatomy
   sections above. Locate a chair or platform where you can have
   sex face-to-face with your spouse or regular sexual partner
   as described, or work out an alternative position that will be

comfortable for a few hours. Devise a regular schedule of sessions and begin Tantric sex practice. Journal progress, problems, and solutions along with your experiences. Think of this as an adventure into the unknown.

2. Watch the movie *Dangerous Beauty*. Note the parts of the film where Egos conflict and the parts where Ego drops away during Ecstasy. Note how conventional morality and religion can be cruel, and what society considers immoral can reflect true love and caring for others. If you were God, which would you prefer?

CHAPTER 10

TANTRIC TRANSFORMATIONS

"If we could change ourselves,
the tendencies of the world would also change."
—MOHANDAS GANDHI

The attitudes and beliefs that determine how we relate to our world are housed in our Egos, our life plans for dealing with the people and things around us. Because these life plans are mere habitual behavior patterns that we learned, they can be changed. Those of us who are on a spiritual Path have signed up for change, to transform from who we are now to a better version of ourselves, closer to our ultimate human potential. We want to be more loving, happier, healthier, and more successful. In Medieval times we might have said we want to be free from sin, from evil.

However the word "sin" in Old English was a translation from an original Hebrew archery term that meant "to miss the mark," to fail to hit the center of the target one is aiming for. So instead of using the word sin, the translators should have used words that mean some of our actions fall short of what a sentient Universe would like from us. Rather than sin damning us to eternal hell, instead we missed the point; we failed to hit the center of the target God set for us.

Remember that to supercharge our spiritual progress, Tantra takes whatever we have and transforms it into progress on our Path. Now that we know that all behavior and attitudes can change, and that sin originally meant not measuring up to desired behavior and attitudes, we can consider some suggestions for using Tantra to transform what we call in the West "the seven deadly sins" into something beneficial. The Western religions usually just give us the list and say, "Don't commit any of these mortal sins." Not very helpful. Tantra tells us how.

✕ LUST: In the previous chapter we noted that Lust is Plan A, sex for personal pleasure. Sex for personal pleasure is fun, and it is possible to develop an addiction for it, something that "misses the mark" by consuming time that we could put to better use, and has the potential to harm ourselves and others. In the prior chapter we outlined how Tantra can transform sex into a transcendent activity. Sex can awaken our Divine Souls, which are part of the Source of unconditional Love for all. Tantra can transform sex from Lust to Love.

✕ WRATH: Anger is potentially very dangerous. Uncontrolled anger can drive us to kill or put us in situations where we are killed. The daily news is full of such stories. A form of sustained anger directed at people, groups of people, or even things, hate is known to cause health problems for the hater. In Buddhism, hate is said to be like drinking poison yourself and expecting the other person to die.

Why would we want to transform anger or hate into love or forgiveness? Why not use anger to punish the one who causes the anger, the conventional way to deal with anger? First realize that no one outside ourselves creates any of our emotional states; it all happens inside our own brain. We receive sensory information from outside ourselves, interpret the information, and then create our own emotional states based on our interpretation of what the incoming sensory information means to us. So no one makes us angry or hateful; we do that ourselves.

We can then deal with our self-created anger in three ways. We can try to change the other person so they no longer do the things that feed our self-created anger, or we can change our own internal transactions that result in our emotional state, or we can just stay angry. Staying angry is a dangerous emotional state that harms us physically and can trigger instinctive attack behavior that can harm us (if we lose the fight) or the "guilty" person (whom we may love), or even innocent people who may get in the way or act as substitute targets, scapegoats. It is too harmful or dangerous to stay angry, which creates an obligation to do something; so let's rule out staying angry and concentrate on the other two options. We must either change the other person or change ourselves.

The first step in changing the other person is to merely let the person know that they caused you to become angry, what made you angry and why. To be accurate, you should say something like, "Maybe it's just me, but when you cut in front of me I couldn't help getting angry." They can either apologize or not. You can either retaliate or forgive. When you retaliate, you are trying to change the other person. Every experienced human should realize how difficult it is to change another person and how low is the chance of success.

It is much easier for you to change your own internal emotional state, because you have, or should have, complete control over your thoughts about what happens to you. In the example of the one who cuts in line, instead of obsessing about how you will arrive ten seconds later for the show, reflect on how it must suck to be someone that everyone hates, and then forgive their action out of pity. Because forgiveness relieves us of the obligation to change the other person, freedom is your reward for forgiveness and your incentive for learning how to forgive.

ANGER HAS ITS USES. IT unleashes the beast in all of us that used to help us fight off lions, tigers, and bears, and such. Like Love, the power of anger can be used to speed our journey on the Path. To realize this, remember times when you were angry, and what anger did during those times. One function of anger is to sharpen attention. This can aid Mindfulness meditation. Anger focuses perception on the cause of the anger and shuts out distractions. Many people know that to solve a problem it helps to become angry with it, and this marshals physical and mental abilities to solve the problem. For example, if you find yourself falling asleep during meditation, you may find becoming angry helps you stay awake. This is especially useful if you practice driving meditation as mentioned earlier.

But if you find yourself becoming too angry too often, consider turning anger into your Path using a Tantric transformation. Here is one method.

Visualize the world as a nuclear reactor with people as the fuel rods that make power, having both the potential for war or the power to make the world a better place to live. Like radioactive materials that give off two neutrons when hit by one, most people give out more anger than what they were hit with. They are reactors. They feel best when they discharge anger in response to anger. Because Egos are separated from others, Egos feel their own pain far worse than the pain they inflict, so people with active Egos always give out more pain than they get. If you do not believe me, try poking people with a sharp stick, and see what happens.

What happens when you put a bunch of these radioactive people together in a small space? They start reacting with one another, and that space heats up and becomes potentially explosive, like a nuclear pile reaching critical mass.

What keeps a nuclear reactor from exploding like an atomic bomb? Between the fuel rods, engineers insert rods of material called moderators that absorb the excess neutron radioactivity. In a similar way, some people have the capacity to absorb anger without giving more anger back, keeping an interpersonal situation from becoming unstable or explosive. We call these people peacemakers, negotiators, mediators, and moderators. Blessed are the peacemakers for without them we will have war.

As a child I was once involved in a border dispute that pitted my brother and sisters against our neighbors' children. The neighbor children said the property line ran down the center of our driveway, so we could not drive our cars into our garage. This panicked us, and there was a standoff between us at the border. After casting threats back and forth, as the oldest child present I could see the threats escalating, and at the rate it was going would turn to physical violence. My mother used to read the Bible to us at home on Sundays because we hated Sunday school. I remembered Jesus' lessons to love your enemies and treat others as yourselves, and thought the only way that might avoid war was to sit on my anger and walk away with my brother and sisters, which we did. Later we talked to our parents and found the neighbor kids were correct, but we had an easement that let us use the driveway. Fighting was unnecessary and would have led to perpetual conflict, no matter who had won the fight. I was a young scientist and atheist at that time, but I concluded that Jesus was a great man, because what he taught works.

I have moderated escalating anger situations countless times since then, and it never feels good to absorb anger and not react. I learned it dissipates with time if I do not replay it or keep it as a grudge, so just leave the situation and let your body's attack hormones metabolize. This works, but it is the normal slow way to deal with anger.

The Tantric way to deal with anger is to transform the anger Energy into Love Energy and send that back to the angry person. Essentially this is attacking back, but with Love. For example, let's say your spouse is really angry at you. Rather than responding with anger or defensively out of fear, try this. Remember the Love you actually feel for your spouse, and say, "You are so beautiful/handsome when you are angry! I thank God I married you." Then show affection and listen closely to your spouse, and see if that allows for a deeper discussion of the conflict without anger or defensiveness. Also think of creative ways to do the same thing in other situations. Take the harmful Energy, transmute it into Love, and send that back. This satisfies the need to not bottle up anger but transforms the situation, and yourself.

WITHIN OURSELVES, TO BE EFFECTIVE, we do not want to be passive beacons of light. We need to get stuff done, so allow enough anger to sharpen the senses with Mindfulness and focus our powers, but not become so angry that we fuck up. Our internal Energy and moderators are often internal images of our heroes and people we know. Let's indulge in some cultural stereotypes and say your dad was the "get-it-done" energetic guy and your mom was the "don't run in the house" moderator. In some homes it may have been the opposite, with a skydiving mom and an accountant dad. Eastern cultures visualize two types of Energy, male and female, which must be combined in balance to be effective.

So you are working on something in the garage, and let's say a bolt will not budge, so you get a bigger wrench, and your inner dad says, "Pull harder and make that son-of-a-bitch move!" (creative cursing is part of getting most hard jobs done), and at the same time your inner mom says, "Be careful and don't throw the wrench through the wall!" That is male and female Energy in balance within one person, action versus moderation, activation versus inhibition, sympathetic versus parasympathetic, whatever you want to call it.

As an effective person we need to be in balance, adjusting the balance for the job at hand. Too much moderation and we risk falling into depression. Too much energy and we risk uncontrollable rage or mania, which leads to emotional exhaustion and then depression. We must learn to sense our internal state of balance, and when too energetic, invoke our internal moderators, and when too passive, unleash our inner drill sergeants. If there were no people in your life to fill these roles, then read about our cultural archetypes and install some heroes in your mind to serve these functions, peacemakers and action heroes. To be a Tantric master, not only do you have homework assignments; you also need to do outside reading. In fact, you have to transform your entire life into the Tantric Path.

LET'S LOOK AT HATE and see if Tantra can turn hate into love. Many religions and philosophies instruct followers to love everyone, even enemies. This is easier said than done. To have any hope of actually doing this, we need to know the basis of ordinary hate and love. Until we evolve and make our Soul our primary consciousness, love and hate are determined by the Ego. We love those who represent what we like about ourselves, and despise those who remind us of what we reject and suppress in our own nature. We love those who feed our Ego, and hate those who threaten our life plan and world view.

That is why love can turn to hate in the blink of an eye. Someone who has been feeding your Ego suddenly does something that threatens to cut off Ego's supply of life Energy and the constant affirmation that supports Ego. Your friend stops seeing you. Your lover disrespects you or has an affair. Your boss criticizes your work. Nothing really changed inside the other person; the change is almost entirely within you. Suddenly you hate them. If you now see them as monsters, that is you projecting your inner emotional state onto them.

When we hate someone who threatens our Ego's sources of Power or the foundations of its life plan, the hate is within us. Hate's target may notice a change in the way we treat them, but the hate, the wish for harm to the other, the negative emotions and physical changes that go with hate, belong entirely to the hater. Realizing that the basis for hate is entirely within ourselves allows us to change our feelings by changing how we think. We can then calm down and solve any problems in a rational way by discussing issues with the other person or defending ourselves more effectively or seeing them as no threat.

We also love people who represent what we like about ourselves, and despise those who remind us about what we reject and suppress in our own behavior. For example, there is no particular reason why gender or even species should determine who we love or have sex with. Many animals and some humans will hump anything. We have all seen this in dogs and some celebrities, and we may have been amused by it. But if we have a strong, learned cultural bias against any activity that is within our natural ability and inclination, then we will hate anything that threatens to lose our control over that natural impulse. Our Ego, our life plan for interacting with our world, then may try to control the unwanted impulses that we do not accept in ourselves by projecting the source of these impulses onto other people, and then try to suppress these impulses by controlling those outer targets. The more urgent our inner impulses become, the more aggressively we may try to control those outside scapegoats for our inner state. That is why people who are the most vocal advocates for certain cultural standards are often caught violating those standards.

People with different personal or family values do not threaten your values unless they try to impose their values on you. So lighten up and try to be tolerant of others with different views. Give your hate to your Ego that created it, and imagine loving those who threaten your life plans, even if you cannot actually feel love for them. In time you may find your Soul that Loves all creation.

✄ PRIDE: Pride or vanity is one of the mental states that is most destructive of efforts to reach our ultimate potential. The first problem with pride is that it creates the idea that we have already attained something valuable and thus hardens our resistance to change. If you are not already healing the sick, feeding the masses, and dazzling all who hear you with the power of your words, then you have a way to go before you reach the highest human potential, and you have no reason to stop learning and stop evolving. I suspect Moses, Buddha, Jesus, Muhammad, and other great masters continued to learn and grow their whole lives on earth.

Pride has several meanings. The one we are most worried about, to exalt one's personal attributes, achievements, or possessions, is a trick by Ego to protect itself from change. Ego is saying, "Look how great I am!" in some aspect. Ego exalts itself to fool us into thinking change is not needed, that we would lose some wonderful quality, if Ego were altered in any way. Ego will even kill or let the body be killed to inflate its view of itself as important, as seen in suicide bomber and mass shooter incidents. They take pride in martyrdom and becoming famous. We will call this Pride capitalized. What greater godlike role could one assume than taking for oneself the power of death over others?

The biggest danger of Pride is the thought that you are superior to others, that you are exalted and deserve special privileges not granted to others, giving license to the thought that you deserve a better life than others because of your virtues. This is also the basis of one of the pitfalls of religions, the belief that its followers are uniquely special or chosen and may rightfully ignore or even kill those who have different beliefs. This version of Pride is really the Ego tricking us into thinking it does not have to change or let go of the Soul's support.

The common antidote for Pride is to cultivate humility or modesty. But except for religious leaders and contemplatives, deprecating oneself or one's qualities does not play well in the West, where we typically have to sell ourselves and our skills in order to stay employed or to discourage detractors. Also, a pitfall with deprecating oneself is to see oneself as too hopeless to improve, which is another trick used by Ego to avoid change.

We also must not allow Pride to feed our Egos. I have heard there are monks and nuns who take Pride in their humility, so that is not the transformation we are looking for. The underlying realization that we must cultivate is that we all hold equal positions in relation to the greater Universe. Speaking poetically, we are all equal in the eyes of God.

So what is the Tantric transformation of Pride? First we will clarify the difference between pride as commonly used and Pride capitalized. It is okay to take pride in something you have done well, as long as you follow that thought with the realization that you could have done even better. This encourages further evolution on the road to your ultimate potential.

The Tantric antidote for Pride is to realize that what our advantages actually give us is the obligation to help others less fortunate. The strong support the weak, in effect being servants to the weak. Note that servants are stronger than their supposed "masters." For example, if the rich were really superior, they could clean their own damn houses. Who is stronger, children or their parents who transport, feed, and clothe them? Think about that. The Tantric transformation of Pride that we want to achieve is to keep healthy pride in our accomplishments, but to see that we are obligated to use what we do well to help others.

Consider this. Suppose a great business person who earns a hundred million dollars per year donates ten million of that to build a new wing to a hospital. In a nearby street, a homeless man with a dollar in his pocket gives that dollar to another homeless person to buy food. Clearly the millionaire will be helping more people both for jobs during construction of the hospital wing and those patients whose lives will be extended. But in terms of level of commitment or devotion to others, who is superior?

If you said the homeless person, or even if you said the millionaire, then you have not been paying attention. We are all equal; no one is superior. That was a trick question. On the Western Tantric Path of Ethics, we are doing our best to help others and are hoping that a conscious and caring Universe notices and sends us signs that help us find our way to a more profound life. In the above example, we do not really know their states of mind. The millionaire may have risked more with that donation, or the homeless man may have loved more with that gift. We really do not know. Generally it is easier for a poor person living close to disaster to see the workings of a caring Universe, but the rich one may be paying closer attention or have less Ego attachment to the result. The important part is to do the best you can with what you have to help others without Ego-feeding Pride, and see what happens.

✄ GLUTTONY: The modern term for Gluttony is Addiction, the inability to limit the use of a substance or behavior, and the term is far broader now than it was even fifty years ago. Now we recognize that a person can be Addicted to almost anything, including excessive food, alcohol, drugs, sex, work, gambling, electronic games, social media, and many other things. The root of all of these Addictions is a dysfunctional Ego, also known as an Addictive Personality, a life plan that misidentifies a need and tries to fulfill that need with something that does not actually meet that need. There are as many different unfulfilled needs as there are people on this planet, so describing how to identify and overcome every unfulfilled need is an impossible task. We will describe ways to overcome one type of Addiction and hope the method can be adapted to overcome others. Alcohol and drug Addictions are well-addressed in various twelve-step programs, so we will not try to duplicate those here. Let's take a look at food Addiction and see if Western Tantra practices can transform that into something beneficial.

There is nothing wrong with eating or enjoying what we eat, but eating too much or choosing the wrong foods destroys the

Body. The Body is our vehicle for learning from Reality, so we can use that learning to achieve our ultimate potential. If we cannot move well, we are limited in where we can go and how long we live. When we lived in caves, if we could not run, some predator would eat our fat ass. Even now, obesity makes us prone to disease and limits our ability to defend ourselves and find a mate. The same goes for Addiction to dieting, making us too thin, if it also makes us weak and prone to disease. There is a middle way which I will call the functional Body, a Body working the way evolution shaped us.

So if you are reasonably healthy and can walk a mile, climb stairs, lift your kids or grandkids, dance all night, and attract and keep a mate, then your Body is functional, and if some asshole says you are too fat or too thin, tell them to fuck off. But if you are weak and sick, then you have to recognize you have a problem, the first step in overcoming an Addiction. Then you have to do something about it, which is easier said than done.

The villain, as with most problems, is our Ego, our Enemy Within, which carries our behavior patterns and Body image. Instead of blaming your genes or parents or metabolism or God or whatever excuse your Ego can come up with to deflect blame from itself and evade responsibility, instead lay the problem on its author. Start by visualizing your Ego as a mountain covering your Heart center, your True Nature, your Divine Soul located in the center of your chest. Every time you experience difficulty or pain resulting from the Addiction, give that pain to the thing that caused it, the mountain that is your Ego covering your True Nature. See the heartaches and pain as strong wind or acid rain that beats on the mountain, eroding it to wash or blow it away from your Soul. The reason to see your Ego as an obscuring mountain is because wearing it away will take time. Like a mountain on earth that is eventually worn down to nothing by wind and water over the passage of time, Ego will erode away as long as you continue to send all your difficulties and pain to the Ego that created them.

ONCE YOUR OLD EGO IS weakened you have two options. One is to create a new life plan without the Addictive behavior. This works best if you can identify the True need which the Addiction does not satisfy. For example, I was a first child with an inexperienced mother and did not get held or nursed enough, because nothing stopped my crying. A baby's first experience of love is from being held and nursed, so I grew up with a love deficit which I tried to satisfy with oral craving. For me food is love. Fortunately, I had a high metabolism, and my mother fed us only healthy foods. We were not allowed any candy or sodas, so I did not gain weight. My thumb, fingernails, gum, blades of grass, and grasshoppers all had low calories, so what I put in my mouth did not make me fat, but if I had had access to what most kids in the West have, I certainly would have become obese.

Now as a divorced adult with kids moved away and no dog, I still have the love deficit, but personal insight and the Tantric methods to erode Ego have given me more effective ways to deal with love hunger. Now when I eat, I visualize food as love and eat Mindfully, enjoying every morsel with intensity. This method substitutes quality of sensation for quantity. If you can focus well on one bite of food, it can serve the same psychological function as ten bites consumed mindlessly. My life plan for eating also includes good nutrition, and lately counting calories, as age slows my metabolism. So this is an example of developing a healthier Ego in relation to eating.

The second more difficult but more universal option to overcome Addiction is to continue eroding away the Ego in order to discover our hidden Soul, the Godhead within, our Divine nature that is connected to God, the source of unconditional Love. Uniting with the sentient, caring Universe gives us strength to overcome almost anything. Unconditional Love satisfies many of our unmet needs, and this may be the True need we are trying to fill when we are trying to overcompensate for something missing in our lives using an Addiction. Who needs anything to excess when we have unconditional Love? This may be similar to the eleventh step in some twelve-step programs, just a different way of reaching it using Tantra.

✂ **GREED:** Greed is taking for yourself more resources than you need for your own use, or if there is plenty for everyone, taking more than your fair share. Greed in an individual seems to be unlimited, so even in the affluent West, if all the greedy people took what they wanted, there would not be enough for everyone. In fact greedy people have done just that, and there are many people in the West in desperate need. I may be getting cynical in my old age, but my life observation is that in any group of a thousand or so, there will be at least one person who will try to take everything, leaving the rest of us with nothing.

   Greed does not actually benefit the individual, because by definition, Greed is keeping more than the person needs, and it carries a huge downside risk. I once asked a man earning in the lower quarter of income what he would do if someday the rich had so much of the country's wealth that he could no longer feed his family, and they were starving. He said, "No problem, I'd just kill a rich person, and take all his shit!" So that is the downside risk of Greed; if you keep more than you need, someone in need may take everything you have, even your life.

To transform Greed, we need to know the causes. I can think of two. One cause is Ego thinking it is privileged and deserves more than others. This is Pride, and we covered transforming that earlier. The other cause for Greed is fear, the fear that we will not have enough for ourselves, so we hold a larger reserve of resources than we may actually need. The root cause of this fear is distrust in the Universe to provide what we need. If we believe in a sentient Universe that cares what happens to us, we will not fear running out of what we need. So if you fear not having enough, then you do not believe in God, as we have defined that term. If you fear not having enough, you have given God a vote of no confidence, regardless of your expressed belief. If you label yourself an atheist, then of course you should have no confidence. Either way, if you would *like* to have confidence in a caring Universe or are just curious to find out, then try the Western Tantric practices of giving, and see what happens.

As stated earlier, one of the main objectives of Western Tantra is to discover if the Universe is sentient and cares about us, so this entire Path is about how you discover this for yourself. The Western Tantric Way to learn if God exists is altruism, benefiting others so that God (if there is one) will manifest to you. So the way to transform from Greed is to see yourself as its opposite, and act as if you are already altruistic. This is the Tantric Way, to visualize the way you want to be, and act as if you already are that way.

If you start passing on what you do not need to others, I predict that long before you run out of what you need for yourself and your family, the sentient Universe that cares will show you that it will provide for you. But do be careful and responsible. Remembering Karma, there may be a long backlog of stingy in your circle of Karma. So build up to altruism slowly, and keep an emergency reserve until you start seeing results. Eventually as you give away, more will be provided and you may find yourself acting as a conduit for passing on to others. Eventually if you experience a windfall, you will automatically ask the Universe to whom you are supposed to give this, and those who need what you were given will appear.

SLOTH: Nobody outside of church ever uses this word in the West, so we will call this Laziness. To convert Laziness into action, try reflecting on this.

Our body and brain are our chief teachers in life. Our body gets us to places of learning and experiences pain when we screw up. Our brain learns from the experience of other people. Body and brain send these lessons learned to the Soul, the Heart-Mind, which is monitoring what the body and brain are doing. In this way, body and brain teach the Soul wisdom, what humans have learned over the millennia: how the world works, how to manage our life, how to care for others, and how our actions have helpful and harmful consequences.

Eventually we learn that our human life has a duration, and if we want this life to have meaning, and if we want to learn what wise men and women say about what happens at the end of life, then we do not have time to waste. If we put off accomplishing our life's purpose and learning how to face death, we may find we have waited too long.

We cannot be sure how long we will live. Accidents and illnesses happen. We may have a life-shortening genetic defect. Even if we live a normal lifespan, the body or brain may become disabled so that we cannot reach places of learning or be able to learn when we get there. We may become blind or deaf or too wracked by pain to concentrate. Or the brain may lose short-term memory so that we only have the information from earlier days to work out the Path to Ultimate Reality and take it to Heart.

I once sat at a dinner table with a woman who had just had a close call from a heart attack. I had never met her before. She remarked to her friend sitting next to her that it really made her think about what she wanted to do with her life. She said to her friend, "I think I will learn to play golf." I hope you can come up with a better plan than that.

The Eastern Tantric Way to combat Laziness is to sit in a graveyard and contemplate the mortality of the body. Although I do this annually as a Buddhist practice, I cannot see this method catching on in the West. In the West we do not need creepy practices. How about this: whenever you see death on the news, say to yourself, "That could have happened to me." Then resolve to finish your life's work without wasting time, and collect information about the life beyond this one while you still can. If you find there is something you need to do, do it. It is better to finish early and then wonder what to do with the rest of your life than suddenly realize you are out of time.

✂ ENVY: Envy is resenting the advantages possessed by another person and wishing to have what they have. At its core, Envy is a person's wish to take a benefit or quality away from the person who has it and to possess that same benefit or quality for themselves. In the realm of thought, this is the same as theft, even if not consummated in the physical world. It does carry the danger that given the opportunity, the envious person will actually take what is coveted, either by force or by manipulating the law, as some wealthy or unscrupulous people are known to do. The danger is well illustrated in the movie *Ladyhawke*.

I have never really understood the wish to actually take things away from another. The only time I ever stole something valuable (scrap brass to make a cannon), I felt so guilty afterwards that I had to sneak it back where I found it, even though the owner never would have missed it. But I do know Envy. To be honest, I Envy the advantages of others regularly, especially when I see a man with a better physique. I toy with the wish to swap bodies, but then immediately think how hard the man must have worked to get that physique and how great a shock it would be for him to suddenly find himself in my body if a consciousness swap were possible. I always realize that if I had decided in my youth to develop my body rather than my brain, I could have had a body like that, and I reflect that it would be cheating to keep the advantages I worked for and also take the ones he worked so hard for, even if I could. This whole Envy and rejection of Envy reflection takes mere seconds, and my use of reflection on compassion and ethics to overcome Envy is a very primitive method that does not display a very high level of spiritual advancement on my part.

The true Tantric transformation of Envy into the Path is to be able to rejoice in the advantages of others, to feel joy for their good fortune without even a hint of a wish to take their advantages for yourself. The Tantric method for doing this is full destruction of the Ego, to let go of Ego completely and become selfless. Techniques for overcoming Ego are found in several chapters. The main technique is merely to realize that Ego is a created fiction, and let it go. When this has been accomplished, it removes the artificial boundary that Ego places between itself and others, and we can come into full union with the rest of the world around us. Then the joy of others becomes your joy, and there is no longer any need for exclusive possession. Everything that belongs to the world is also yours. This is my wish for you, that all-that-is be yours.

HOMEWORK:

1. Watch for the occurrence of any of the seven deadly sins. Which are your favorites? If you said none, you are probably fooling yourself. Kick your Ego in the ass and try again. Then try out the techniques for overcoming each of your favorite deadly sins. Write down the results in your journal.

2. Find the movie *Ladyhawke*. Set aside an evening to watch it. I am a film buff, and movies are an art form that we regularly abuse. They are meant to be seen as a continuous experience while paying attention, not interrupted every few minutes to get food or refreshments and see why the dog is barking. So set aside a time to really pay attention, and take no more than one intermission near the middle of the film. During the viewing, notice how envy can lead to ruin, how established religion may be more about power than love, and how those rejected by society may better reflect true religion than the mainstream.

FURTHER READING:

If you have an Addiction, read a guide on overcoming that Addiction. Addictions are among the most limiting afflictions humans can have, shortening your life and bringing pain to loved ones. You must learn to overcome Addiction before much Tantric progress is possible.

CHAPTER 11

TANTRIC TOOLS

*"We shape our tools, and thereafter
our tools shape us."*

—UNKNOWN

I n this chapter, we will provide a set of Tools that Western Tantric practitioners can use to enhance certain steps on the Path of Ethics or to overcome specific problems. As an engineer, builder, and mechanic, I value a good set of Tools for designing, building, and maintaining a Tantric Vehicle. The ones you decide to use become your Western Tantric Toolbox.

 JOURNALING: We are limited creatures, and we remember only about a quarter of what we first learn when presented with new information. To get closer to one hundred percent recollection takes repetition, as all of you who have memorized speeches, song lyrics, or your lines in a play know. Likewise, you will have

to read this book more than once to pick up most of the meaning. The same goes for spiritual realizations or interesting events that happen as a result of your Tantric practice. You will not remember most of them unless you write them down as they happen.

I recommend keeping some sort of journal or other written record to record your Tantric progress and key events. I note dates of interesting dreams or events in an appointment book and reference those entries to longer descriptions on 3x5 cards or larger sheets of paper. I like paper records, because paper is available everywhere, and no one wants to steal it. But the notepad function on your smartphone or tablet would also work, if you remember to back it up at least weekly, and never let it out of your sight for more than a tenth of a second.

Also when journaling, you are noticing how the acts of others lead to consequences, and this provides helpful lessons. It helps us develop what Buddhists call "the long view." Most people think in the short-term, looking at immediate results the way a child throws a tantrum and gets candy. If you record events, you can see the results of Karma in the longer term. For example, no one invites the parents of the spoiled child to their house because they do not want the brat there, but the parents don't remember the broken items or their promises to repay.

Journaling is very useful because memory fades and distorts with time. Events you thought happened together may have occurred days or months apart. I often have years when I think not much was happening, but when I look back at my notes I realize much happened that I had forgotten. Sometimes events are remembered but important details are lost. Names of people you thought were part of memories are lost or changed by memory. Things will happen when you practice Tantra, and it may be important to look back and reread about past events as your perspective changes.

For example, a friend of mine told me about a dream he had about being underwater in a deep ocean trench near the Marianas and seeing an earthquake cause a huge underwater landslide which created a tidal wave killing many people. We looked at the area on a map, and I recorded his dream in an email. About nine months later an earthquake caused an underwater landslide in an ocean trench west of Banda Aceh, resulting in the huge tsunami which killed thousands. I was able to use my written record to see that his dream approximately matched that event and could prove that the dream preceded the event.

Dream memories are the most ephemeral, in my opinion, because many arise from the Soul rather than the human brain. When the brain has a thought, it is recorded in memory, but dreams seem to evaporate as soon as you stop thinking about them. So I keep pen and paper near my bed to record dreams, because by the time electronic devices are located and boot up and insist on updating themselves, the dream has already faded. In that brief moment between sleep and waking, my body can write before my brain fully wakes up. I cannot work electronic devices until I am fully awake, which seems to suppress the dream memory. One night I had a series of dreams that must have occurred over a period of hours, and which I completely forgot upon waking until I came across my notes days later. The dream sequence was very profound, and I would have lost it completely if I had not recorded the dreams as they happened.

I have also noticed that what seems like a short dream or profound waking thought sometimes takes pages to write down. This provides a clue about how our Soul or other Divine beings may communicate in brief packets of information containing a lot of information when "unpacked." In information science this is known as "burst transmission." In spiritual lingo it is called "instant knowing" and is a sign that a message or idea has a Divine origin and is genuine. Writers often get an entire novel from one dream, and scientists often wake up with the answer to a difficult question that baffled them for days beforehand.

So write stuff down so that you can go back later and be amazed. Our lives are much more interesting than what we remember later, after memory is sanitized by time.

✂ PRAGMATISM: For those more philosophical than religious who need a Base philosophy, Pragmatism seems compatible with Western Tantra and might serve. Pragmatism is an American philosophical movement founded by C. S. Pierce and William James in the late 1800s. Pragmatism posits that the meanings of concepts are to be determined by their practical utility, that the function of thought is to guide action, and that truth is to be tested by the practical consequences of belief. My knowledge of Pragmatism is newly acquired and very limited, but I think this means that to determine what is true, apply it and see what happens. If ideas do not work or function as expected, adjust what you think is true and see if the new ideas work better or worse. Eventually you will have a view of reality that is effective in guiding action.

For example, if you think illegal aliens are bad people and make the country worse, and you think this is important, then you must meet some illegal aliens and apply your tests of "good and bad" to see if your ideas are correct. I met a few and found them to be no different than the rest of us, and they had jobs and were not a burden on social systems, so I do not support efforts to remove them as a practical matter. By not worrying about their effect on the nation, we have time and resources for other activity.

Pragmatism rejects the idea that thought is a mirror of reality, but holds instead that thought is a tool for prediction, problem solving, and action. Philosophy is best judged for its practical utility and successes. For example, if one holds nihilistic beliefs that cause one to become depressed and suicidal, then the utility of these beliefs is low. Whereas if one holds Tantric views and does meditation that makes one happier and more successful in dealing with work and family, then that philosophy has more practical utility, whether or not it is closer to reality.

Some key concepts of Pragmatism include: no beliefs are privileged (cast in stone), "truth" means useful to believe, there is more than one way to view the world, and a theory should be tested by how well it explains and predicts. Western Tantra appears to be compatible with this philosophy.

HEALTHY DOUBT: Western Tantra is not a faith-based belief system. As stated in an earlier chapter, there are too many huge gaps in human knowledge to be absolutely certain of anything. Rather than "lock-in" concepts of life, the afterlife, a particular form of deity, or methods to reach goals, or even the goals themselves, keep an open mind and a healthy sense of doubt that you have all the answers. Test reality with altruistic acts and see what is revealed to you. Develop confidence based on your own experiences, but always realize that human limitations mean your views can never be exactly right, and be ready to let go of ideas when reality differs from what you thought or wished. Reality is not all bad. Most of my encounters with reality showed it to be better than I ever could have imagined. In fact a problem with reality may be that some aspects of it seem to be too good to be true.

Testing concepts of reality should be like testing equipment for mountain climbing. You need to be confident enough in your equipment to have the courage to make the climb, but have enough doubt in the equipment and your ability that you remain careful and have backups and alternatives if something fails. Likewise on the Path, you must be confident enough in what you are doing to proceed, but not so confident in any particular method or so sure of any particular result that you miss an opportunity or quit when something you were sure would work fails. Be flexible and ready to change, but confident enough to proceed.

✂ THREE ASPECTS OF EXPERIENCE: When events happen, especially difficult ones, how do we know that God, the sentient Universe, knows we are here and cares about us? This *Western Tantra* book proposes that all your life experiences will have three aspects: a test, a lesson, and a gift; signs that the Universe is sentient and cares what we are doing. If we can find the three aspects of significant events, then we should eventually gain confidence that what is happening to us is not random. The test, lesson, and gift will not necessarily always be in that order. Let's look for them in a common life experience.

So let's say that your child falls ill on Friday. "That's bad," says Ego. "I have stuff to do at work," says brain. Seeing your child sick and miserable, your heart goes out to her, and you wish you could take the illness from her. You call your boss and tell him you will stay home with your sick kid. You make your child comfortable, feed her soup, read her favorite stories, and spend the day with her. She says she loves you. She gets better over the weekend. You make up some work time on Sunday. The next Monday your boss criticizes you for taking a day off at a critical time for the department. You tell him you partly caught up on Sunday and will work late tonight, but your boss is still angry at you. What are the three aspects of this experience?

These will depend on the people involved, but let's speculate. The test may have been, "Will you set aside your wishes to help someone in need?" You did; you pass. The lessons may have been that helping others builds strong relationships, and your boss is just using you to get his job done and cares nothing about you or your family. Maybe it is time to look for a new job. I see a few gifts in this example. Your Heart opened to your child's pain, showing you that your Heart works, giving confidence you can rely on it. You also got to spend time with your child while she is growing up; the event happened on a Friday, minimizing lost work time, and your daughter said she loves you and meant it. A passed test, two valuable lessons, and four priceless gifts, all from an event that would be described as "bad" and to be avoided.

I think by consistently looking for the three aspects of experience in your life events, eventually you may learn why you are here, experience the full extent of life, and grow from it. If you can always find these three elements in every experience, what does it say about our life on earth?

✂ PRAYER: Prayer is not the primary tool on the Path of Ethics. According to the Western Tantric views, we are all part of a sentient Universe that already cares about us, knows what all of us need, and will give us what is best for us whether we ask or not. Even a human will attend to a cut finger. The finger does not have to pray to the brain for help; the brain knows the finger's pain, and the whole body moves to help the finger. If you think we must pray to God for help, then you must think God is dumber than humans. But prayer is known to help heal us physically and help us cope, so the act itself is beneficial. To be honest, I pray daily to fulfill Tantric commitments, and whenever anyone asks me to pray for someone, I do. So if we are going to pray even if it is unnecessary, let's look at how to do it well.

The typical Western prayer does not do it well. It starts with complimenting God as if God has an Ego that needs affirmation. Sometimes we debase ourselves to elevate God far above us, as if God needs elevating. Then we ask God for what we want, as if we know what is best for us. Sometimes we just order God to give us what we want, as if God is our servant. Often we throw in what we will do to please God if God will but grant our wishes, as if we can bargain with God. If we promise to refrain from sin if God does what we want, does that mean we intend to continue sinning if God does not grant our prayer? And if we never kept our bargains before, do you think God believes us now? Try crossing out all of the above unnecessary or offensive elements in a typical Western prayer and see what you are left with. I once tried this to find an effective example of a Western prayer but had to look to Buddhism to find a prayer without these elements. A typical Buddhist prayer goes something like this, "Please help me become better so that I can help others better."

Let's see if we can find prayers that work. In my youth I prayed a lot, but none of my requests were granted. They were all things or conditions I wanted for myself, and to be brutally honest, I did not really need them. Selfish wishes seldom come true. During my atheist phase in my twenties, and faced with what I thought was a life-threatening illness, I prayed for a cure; and it was granted through people in an improbable series of events with a remarkable outcome. It was a Miracle as defined earlier. From this I learned I was a lousy atheist, because the first time I was in really deep trouble, I prayed.

Now I once again pray often, and here are my lifetime observations of what works and what does not. What separates us from harmony with the Universe is the Ego belief that we are separate from the rest of the Universe. So benefits that feed the Ego, making it stronger, will not be granted. Selfish prayers do not work. Prayers that harm others will not be granted, even if we think that is beneficial. If you do this and the prayer is answered, it is either coincidence or you are praying to the wrong guy. For example, if praying for money for an addict could kill that person, God would not grant this prayer. We are here to grow and learn, not necessarily to have an easy life.

I learned that the Universe works through people and natural processes in ways we could never imagine, that the objective of prayer must be important, that the Universe does not care what your belief system is, and what is given is what is needed, not what we think is needed. God does not take orders from us.

My usual prayer now is almost always, "Lord, please do what is best for this person." This prayer has always been granted, as far as I can determine. Your life experiences may differ from mine, but this is what I find that works. And I do not believe for a minute that God needs me to tell God what needs doing. That would be Ego at work. Here is what I think is happening in prayer. I think the Universe is holding its breath hoping someone will pray, so that the Universe can inspire the one who prays a valid prayer by granting it. Prayers are granted to teach us Love. God will help those in need whether anyone prays or not.

Lately I started another kind of prayer as I realized at least part of what the Universe has done to protect and grow me through adversity. When we are suffering, it is hard to feel thankful.

Because of this, what God does not typically get from us is gratitude, so maybe we should try to find things to be thankful for. God knows what we do for others, but maybe God does not know that we see what God does for us. So my new prayer is simply, "Thank you Lord." Sometimes it is, "Thank you, thank you, thank you, thank you, thank you......"

✂ HEALING TOUCH: When you encounter someone in distress, do not stand distantly from them as you try to comfort them. Touch them in an appropriate location. Imagine Love flowing from your Heart to where you are touching them. Western science has established that human touch is beneficial. It can improve mood and speed healing. Hugs are even better. And do not wait for people to be in distress. Touch more.

✂ REPROGRAMMING: In the computerized West, we now think of many life activities the way we think of our computers, interfacing with others, uploading, downloading, and so forth. The written and spoken word has long been a method by which knowledge gained by one person is passed to another person. Human civilization is built on this method for sharing and storing knowledge. Think of written and spoken words as sharing data between human brains, which are like computers.

Think of Tantra as software for reprogramming how the human brain works. However, unlike silicon computers where software is uploaded once, our human brains, our organic computers, are more flexible than the ones we build. We filter what we bring in and forget what is not used to save space for what we do use or what seems relevant at the time. To really learn Tantra, we have to use what we learn and reread the words as we evolve. Some instructions may not seem relevant when we first see them, and we only retain about a quarter of what we read on the first pass. This means we have to reread the *Western Tantra* text periodically as we forget and change from what we were to what we will become.

The entire body of human knowledge is like this. We can read and reread and reprogram ourselves and change. This means that no matter how deficient our upbringing and no matter how poor our life plan is at achieving happiness, we can link to the human body of knowledge and reprogram our mental computers to work better, if we can read or hear, and if we have the freedom to access what we need to know.

We are fortunate to live in the enlightened West where we can access five thousand years of human knowledge. Pity the poor people living in restrictive societies that have limited written and oral memories because they burn books, destroy art and music, kill teachers, and persecute those with different views. That is the true poverty of some non-Western countries and of subcultures within the West that ban knowledge outside of their narrow beliefs.

We all come from different backgrounds and are at different levels of spiritual maturity, so what each of us needs to complete ourselves is different. As long as we are not harming others, let no one tell us what we need to know or believe.

✄ MUSIC: Eastern Tantra has its chanting, very inspiring when chanted in Tibetan. The theory behind chanting is that the vibrations produced stimulate the Energy centers in the Spirit Body to assist with the process of awakening our True Nature. Unfortunately, chanting in English (possibly any Western language) sounds to Westerners like the mind control used by autocratic governments to control the masses. Maybe we have seen too many movies about evil dictators and their minions. We recoil from the message because chanting in a language that we understand sounds sinister.

Fortunately, in the West we have a way of delivering poetry and inspiring vibrations straight to the Soul in a form we can accept. We call it music. Not all music inspires, of course. But some music and lyrics—wow!

A common theme in music is love that lasts forever. If you think about it, what kind of love on Earth lasts forever? Most partners end up either divorced or staying together out of habit. I know there are humans who truly love one another for their entire lives, but be honest, these are rare jewels. And even these loves do not last forever. The partners die. Yet we know in our Hearts that eternal love is possible, which is why songs of eternal love resonate with us. Why?

Go back to the earlier chapters and see where artists get their inspiration. The well of creativity is in the formless Divine realm. There and only there does unconditional eternal Love exist. So when the lyricists dip into the well of creativity to describe the love they feel for their lovers, the water they come up with is our connection to God, the Source of Love. Yes, we will experience true Love. The lovers will experience this Love when they are united with the conscious Universe, with God. Only then can Love be eternal.

Read the Song of Songs and listen to popular love songs. Ask yourself this: can the words realistically apply to ordinary human love, or is the lyricist actually reflecting God's Divine Love for us? Observe how the composer's melody stirs the Soul. Music with spiritual content can do for us what chanting does for Easterners. Listen to more music; that is a Western Tantric Tool.

"If a man does not keep pace with his companions, perhaps it is because he hears a different drummer. Let him step to the music which he hears, however measured and far away."
—Henry David Thoreau, *Walden*

✂ DIVERSITY AND CHANGE: Because we are like children in the world, we feel more comfortable with people around us who are like us. People who are different from us threaten our confidence in our life plans, especially if those people with different appearances and values are doing better than we are. This was the case in Germany prior to the Second World War. With their strong interpersonal ties, belief in education, and work ethic, the Jewish minority population was more prosperous as a group than the majority. The majority resented and persecuted the Jews. When the Jewish scientists fled to the Allies, taking their knowledge with them, it doomed the Axis.

Look at the Middle East. Here in the West we have always been the stronger culture because in the West we believe in diversity and have the creative benefit of many ideas from many cultures. So it is with people who are open and accept ideas from different people and cultures.

Consider eternity. Imagine how boring eternity would be if the universe and everything and everyone in it were the same. Life would quickly become so boring that we would yearn for death. The only reason we wish for sameness now is because our lives are changing too fast for our life plans, our Egos, to keep up with the pace of change. But imagine if everything was uniform and nothing ever changed. Life would no longer be interesting.

Even our Egos can learn to accept diversity and change. More so our Souls, which are stronger, faster, and more adaptable than our Bodies and our Egos. With eternity in mind, diversity and change are not threats to our existence; they are the very spice of existence. Be open to change. Broaden your horizons. Embrace diversity. That is the Western Tantric Way.

⚹ HOMELESSNESS: It is a terrible feeling to be without a home. All of us have at least been temporarily without a home, if only during a move or vacation or natural disaster. Knowing how it feels, we should try to comfort those who are homeless, knowing that it has happened to us and may happen to us again. Helping the homeless is one of the most common and available ways to help others in life-changing and life-saving ways. We can help them directly by providing food, shelter, and warm clothing. Or we can help them indirectly by working through churches or our community to provide aid.

We can become advocates for the homeless. As of 2013, about one in five hundred Americans were homeless, about one homeless person per two hundred families. This shows the level of community support needed. Divide the size of your community by five hundred to see the approximate number of homeless people your community should be caring for. If your community is not supporting that number, and it won't be, then your community is not doing its share. The typical way a community cares for its homeless is by confiscating their "junk" (tents, bedding, cooking facilities, clothing) and dumping the homeless on a nearby, usually poor, community that will not complain as loudly. An always available way of helping others is to become an advocate for low and no-income housing in your community (not someone else's) and helping find ways to feed, clothe, and employ them.

I do not know the extent of the problem in Europe, but it is probably higher than in America because of the refugee crises. Regardless what the extent is, the homeless provide an endless supply of people needing help. All you have to do is search.

If you are threatened with homelessness yourself, use this realization to become disillusioned with the Material world, seeing how harsh and unfeeling it is. Realize the importance for urgency in progressing on the Path. At any moment we could lose the conditions that allow us the time and freedom to transform our lives. With Karma in mind, realize that the best way to avoid homelessness is to help the homeless.

If you are homeless and found this book in the trash or the public library, or it was given to you, notice that when you are shunned and cut off from the rest of society, you are not cut off from a caring Universe. Living near death daily, you see that Miracles save you at critical times. Pity the poor rich people living in gated communities who do not need God, so they do not get to see God at work as you do.

❊ THE WORLD: We are instructed to change the world, our planet Earth, into a heavenly place, and of course we should try to do that. But the Mystics say we will fail in this effort because the Earth, our world, is perfect just the way it is. Why would the Mystics say that when our world is so clearly flawed? Maybe it is because the Mystics know we need its flaws in order to evolve. Let's explore this possibility.

Clearly the people living on planet Earth have flaws. I am only slightly serious when I ask, "What if this world is an asylum and we are its inmates?" Is there any evidence that we humans are insane? Sadly there is abundant evidence. Let's start with "our" planet. It is about four billion years old and weighs about 6×10^{24}

kilograms which is about 120 septillion megatons of TNT equivalent energy converted into matter. Not sure of my math here. What
would it cost in dollars to convert that much Big Bang energy into
the matter that we call Earth? God only knows. Yet we modern
humans, who have been here only a few thousand years, think we
own it, that it is ours by right. Insane.

We could not even afford our own bodies if we had to buy
them from the universe. The Sun, the Earth, and all the creatures
on this planet are gifts. Humans used to know this, but we have
forgotten. And how does modern humanity treat its gifts? The way
we foul our air and water, strip the land and oceans of resources,
and poison our food supplies, we may render the Earth partly
uninhabitable within the lifetimes of people already here, not to
mention future generations. Insane.

How about our governments? Half of them cannot provide
basic needs for their people, and the other half let the people
controlled by the incompetent governments starve, or they build
walls and armies to keep the starving people away from their stuff.
Insane. How about laws that let the rich take more of the Earth's
resources and let the poor fall into subsistence or worse? Insane.
How are minorities treated? Insane. How does history repeat
itself? If insanity is doing the same things over again and expecting a different result, then we are insane.

We know, or at least some of us know, that our purpose on
Earth is to become more like God so that we can become one with
God. Figuratively speaking, if we hate and harm others on Earth,
how can we expect to get along in heaven? For the ethical atheists
out there, how do we become ideal humans who can coexist in
harmony with others to achieve a sustainable future?

What if Earth is a place where we are free to be as horrible
or as wonderful as we wish, so that we can discover for ourselves

what thoughts, words, and deeds work and do not work for getting along with others? Universal Love is the only thing that works universally, and until we learn that, we cannot expect to create heaven in this life or the next. Maybe that is why our world is the way it is. Here we are free to be as loving or as shitty as we want, and by experiencing the consequences, we learn how to be. Use the world to learn.

If that is the way things are, then the world is a perfect place of learning just the way it is. Treat it like a gift. And if it is the perfect place of learning for us, then a conscious and caring Universe or the collective consciousness of the human race will save it from destruction by working through people, through us. We hope. Learn from the world. Teach others what you learn.

What is your part in this? What is the Tantric method? If you would change the world for the better, first make yourself better. That is the Tantric Way.

✖ HONOR AND INTEGRITY: Humans often do not do what they say they will do, feeling that only the written word is binding now in society. That gives people license to say whatever they wish in order to manipulate other humans or just make them go away. We say, "Okay, I will do it tomorrow," or "I gave at the office." We think we are free to think anything, because we think our thoughts are private. We say, "You look lovely darling," while we think, "I should dump the old hag for a younger woman." If your words and thoughts mean nothing in life, what can you possibly do after death to communicate with God and others when thought is all we have? Can you sign a written contract after you have shed your body? How private and non-binding are your thoughts after death? Can you instantly train your thoughts to be truthful in death, when they were always different than your words and deeds in life?

Make your word your bond, and make your actions match your words. This is Honor. We Honor our commitments. And make your thoughts match your words and actions. This is Integrity. People trust those with Integrity. Before paper documents, we had Honor and Integrity. Honor and Integrity will serve us in life and beyond death.

The anonymous Internet bullies expressing their hateful thoughts because they cannot be identified amply demonstrate what life would be like if all we had to communicate were our thoughts. So train your thoughts to match your ethics while you live and have a chance to train your mind, lest you die and spew hate and lies to God and Spirits out of habit from your untrained mind like an Internet bully.

There is another good reason to train your thoughts while you live. Most people know what you are thinking. That is because our body is connected to our brain and communicates our thoughts to those who can read body language, which is most of us. We have to learn to read body language in order to survive and prosper. Those of us with open Hearts are also connected to the world around us and know what others are feeling. If you always think your boss is an asshole, but you do your job well and get fired anyway, now you know why. Make your thoughts match your words and your words match your actions. That is the Western Tantric Way.

HOMEWORK:

1. When significant events happen in your life, both good and bad, write them into your journal. Leave space to write the test, lesson, and gift as you learn what they were. Some aspects may not

be evident until you can look back at the events and see how they changed you.

2. The next time you are presented with a person with problems that are beyond your ability to help with, try the prayer, "Lord, please do what is best for this person." And see what happens.

3. If you have no friends belonging to a cultural group that is well-represented in your area, find some and get to know them socially. If you have a most disliked cultural group, the most Tantric approach would to become close friends with a member of that group.

4. Help a homeless person in some way.

5. Try to discover at least one admirable quality about everyone you deal with frequently. Train your thoughts to at least reflect respect.

FURTHER READING:

The Varieties of Religious Experience by William James reflects the author's Pragmatism philosophy: that religious experiences should be the topic of study of religion, not religious institutions.

The Four Agreements by Don Michael Ruiz is about developing Honor and Integrity. It is a short book that can be read in a few hours.

CHAPTER 12

WESTERN TANTRIC PATHS

"Do you not see how necessary a world of pain and troubles
is to school an intelligence and make it a soul?"

—JOHN KEATS

This is almost the end. We have seen that some aspects of the established religions are unsupported at best and misleading at worst. Yet they contain hidden truths that may apply to this time and place, especially the truth of Love. We have seen that one factor dividing humans is failing to clearly define what we mean when we use spiritual terms, and we have tried to clarify our use of terms for aspects of the Tantric Path.

We have seen that Western Tantra encourages the use of modern scientific methods to shine light on the unseen Spirit and Divine worlds, but we also demonstrated how scientific methods have been used incorrectly to refute religious ideas. We have shown how vast are the gaps in human knowledge, and there is plenty of room in these gaps for Divine beings to actually exist. We have seen how we may even experience Divine beings if we have open minds and are willing to try new approaches to see what happens for ourselves. If we but do the work.

Western Tantra theorized that the entire Universe is conscious and cares about us. To test this, we find we have to care about others to see if the Universe responds to what we do. In order to care about others, we transform ourselves into people who Love and act on that Love to help others in need. If we succeed, we see Miracles—if we learn how to recognize them. We now know that Ego is our enemy in this effort, and we also know how to overcome its limitations and pitfalls.

We looked at Tantric methods and meditations, including sexual practices, and how to use them to transformation what we have into what we need for the Path. And we now have a set of tools which we can use to assist with our transformation from ordinary to transcendent.

The best I can do to conclude this last chapter of *Western Tantra* is to provide some examples of how to apply Western Tantric practices to some aspects of human life. This is applied Western Tantra. Not all methods will apply to all lives, and not all need to be used exactly this way. But they illustrate how Western Tantra can be used to make your entire life the Path. What happens when you do this? Well—that may surprise you, and there is no way I can prepare you for that.

✂ ADVERSITY AS THE PATH: I love listening to the Sunday morning preachers with their messages of hope for a better life. If you have faith and patience, God will bless your life on Earth with abundance, they say. You will hear no such message from me. There is an old parable about blind men examining an elephant as an explanation for the different views of God. I don't remember it exactly, but it goes something like this. Several blind men examine an elephant that they are told is God (must be pretty gullible) and are asked to describe what God is like. The blind man who finds the trunk says God is like a great serpent encircling the world. The blind man who examines the leg says that is not true, God is like the sacred tree of life. The blind man under the belly says, wrong, God is like the heavens above. No, says the blind man examining the elephant's side, God is vast, impenetrable, and immovable. Apparently, I am the blind man standing under the anus.

The Sunday morning preachers are lovely people, and their hearts are in the right place. It is good to have hope that things will get better when times are tough, and they provide that hope. However you do not have to live very long on this planet to see that for some people, even wonderful caring and religious people, life sucks and then they die. Life on earth never provided them the love and material comfort promised by the preachers.

My life observation is that the product of a life well lived is *you*, not rewards you may or may not receive. What do I mean by this? What I mean is that during our time on earth we are being shaped by life. We are products of contact with Reality, in all its forms, both good and bad. Our life on earth is not the end result or reward for good behavior and right attitude. Life on earth is how we are shaped into people with the right attitude who treat others kindly. Life on earth is not our reward; it is the mill, the workshop, the forge, and we are the products of that experience. If we turn out well, God and the world reap the reward, not us. To become a gift to God and the beings on this planet, the entire Universe, that is the Tantric Way.

Pray not for abundance and ease of the material life, which must eventually end. Pray that Reality will shape us into the people God wants us to become, and if we are not quite ready, run us through the mill again until we are. Then take us into union with Totality. That is the way we should pray. That is what we should wish for. That is the Tantric wish.

Let's suppose that you actually want to become a guardian angel, protector buddha, teacher, healer, or other Divine helper in the life after this one. If so, stop bitching about what is happening to you in this life, and prepare yourself as a helper by experiencing the various flavors of people with problems, so that you know how to help them. The most common lie by helpers is, "I know how you feel." You cannot know if you have never experienced their problem. Let's look at the list of human adversity. In the world and even in the West we have: poverty, hunger, unemployment, homelessness, illness, pain, disability, aging, death, loneliness, alienation, obscurity, insanity, addiction, abuse, enslavement, discrimination, persecution, theft, torture, imprisonment, fear, hate, anger, violence, and war. If you are missing any of these experiences, then instead of avoiding them, try to think of a way to fill that gap by doing charity work with those who have experienced those adversities, so that you can learn about them. And do not say, "I know how you feel." Rather ask, "How did that make you feel?"

Think of planet Earth as a boot camp for angels and buddhas and you will not be disappointed with what your life is like. If you do well, the Universe may send you people to help, and you may begin to see what sort of angel or buddha you are being groomed to be. Be in this life what you want to become in the next. Like a good warrior, if things are tough, think, "This just makes me tougher. If it kills me, the Universe must think I'm ready." Of course it is also okay to ask the Universe for a temporary break.

An example of a tough life for a wonderful person that you may be familiar with is Princess Diana. She could have had a life of ease as royalty, but she chose instead to be a true "mum" and change the way royal children are raised. She became the darling of the press, but instead of basking in fame, took on charitable causes. One of her causes was the tragedy of children maimed and killed by unexploded mines in former war zones. No one wanted the danger and cost of removing the mines. When she realized that the press would follow her anywhere, she walked them into an active minefield to talk about the problem and impress upon them the urgency of doing something. Making this problem visible may have influenced funding for the company I worked for, SRI International, to perfect the technology to locate buried mines safely using ground-penetrating radar. Now the West maps and removes these mines. She caught hell from the people around her for her efforts to change things, but she hung tough, and shortly before her death she marveled at how strong she had become. Was her life tragedy or victory? God only knows. All I know is she inspired me.

SUMMARIZING ADVERSITY AS THE PATH, I do not think God has ever deserted anyone, despite appearances. Our view of Reality is limited, but I think what appears to be abandonment and trouble is instead the way we grow through adversity, not with abundance and ease. If your life is tough, rejoice. The Universe has noticed you and is working on you the way one forges a tool to make it stronger. Hang in there and do the best you can, and you may be able to marvel at the change in yourself. So if your life is tough, don't say, "Stop, I've had enough." Say, "I'm still standing. Thanks for your confidence in me. Now can I have a short break, please?" All soldiers need a little R&R now and then.

To be perfectly honest, while I'm being pounded by life the way it is, I really wish I could be living a life of peace and abundance surrounded by loving friends and family. The Sunday morning preachers do give us hope for a better life, and I am sure God blesses them for that.

✂ PAIN AS THE PATH: You may be in pain. I feel for you and wish I could take it away entirely, but that probably would not be good for you. Pain keeps us alert and alive and may even be a gateway to the world beyond this one, or the key that opens the door. This sounds improbable, so let's discuss it. First, we all experience low-level pain all the time, nerves firing into our nervous system. Our brain adjusts to this low-level stimulation and balances it with inhibitory system activity to maintain a certain level of brain activity that allows the brain to work effectively. If the level of stimulation arriving at the brain drops too low, the inhibitory activity dominates, and the brain activity decreases. Subjectively it becomes harder to think, the world seems dull and meaningless, and we say we are depressed. If there is too much incoming stimulation, the brain is out of balance in the opposite direction. Subjectively, the world looks threatening, and we say we are anxious or fearful. If our brain activity is balanced with just enough stimulation but not too much, chemicals are released in the brain that are felt as pleasure, things are "just right." Our plan for ensuring things feel just right is the Ego, our life plan for interacting with our environment.

So the first benefit of pain is that it tells us something has to change. If the pain has a physical source, we may need to find a doctor, change our diet or activity, or rest and recover. Our Ego may have an effective physical recovery plan, or our Ego may be part of the problem. So for example, if Body pain is caused by drug use and the Ego plan for dealing with all pain is to numb it with pain-killers or overwhelm it with pleasurable narcotics, then the Ego is part of the problem and must change. Similarly, if someone grows up abused and marries a partner who abuses, and they stay with that abusive partner because when they leave the abuse, they become depressed from the lack of abusive stimulation, then their Ego plan is part of the problem and must change.

Changing the Ego to make it more effective in dealing with the environment is the subject of psychology and psychiatry, and there are many resources in the West for developing a healthier Ego. There are already a great number of self-help books that will help us do this, and I will not try to duplicate their efforts here.

The Tantric Way is different. The Tantric Way to handle pain and achieve happiness is to choose a Divine mode of being that is not overcome by pain or seduced by pleasure, and to visualize yourself as having attained that mode of being already. Put all your Soul's Life Energy into being what you want to become, and stop feeding your old limited Ego. Stop feeding the way you used to see yourself as a limited human. As you put all your Energy into your new Divine state of being, the old you will eventually waste away and die, leaving only Divine you. What is left is your Soul, which is your True Self. You can verify this for yourself by doing the work.

Allies in this venture are your body and brain, which are honed by millions of years of evolution and are far stronger, adaptable, and more able to heal than our limited Egos give them credit for. It is our Egos that are wimps. As a medical responder, I have seen macho guys scream like little girls when I tried to wash out a small wound or remove a sliver. What the fuck? Bodies have survived bear-mauling! I heard of a guy who was nailed to a cross and still had enough compassion to forgive the people who did it, and to comfort the guys nailed up next to him. To this day, some people find it beneficial to recreate that painful event.

According to many sources, we have within us a Soul which is part of Reality and capable of uniting with ultimate Reality. This Soul survives the death of the Body and may be immortal. It cannot be harmed by anything in the Material world, thus is fearless. Soldiers in war face certain death to defend wounded comrades; prisoners of war volunteer to be executed to save other prisoners; rescuers brave fires and animal attacks to save strangers. Some part of us is strong enough to resist torture and brave enough to face death to benefit others.

The trick is to find our Soul and make it our primary consciousness. To locate it, we have to think like it. We develop the wish to benefit others without letting concerns about endangering ourselves stop us. The Tantric method is to imagine that we already have these qualities, that we are already like this, and then act as someone who has those qualities. This effort is aided by visualizing oneself as one of our cultural archetypes with a known set of qualities that we can use to model our thoughts and actions. In thought and word and deed, we become that archetype in the world.

Choose this archetype carefully. If it does not have the qualities of the Soul you are trying to find, the archetype will just become another Ego identification and will merely feed the beast you should be trying to starve. If you want to become fearless, do not emulate someone who became paranoid, hid within a close circle of friends, killed imagined enemies, and had a distorted view of reality. You will never find your God within that way. That is where belonging to one of the established religions is helpful. Each one has heroic, selfless archetypes, teachers, saints, prophets, buddhas, gods, and goddesses to serve as models. For example, many of the Christian saints saw themselves as the hands of Christ in the world, one with the Savior and continuing his work in the world. In the same way, Eastern Tantric practitioners visualized themselves as emanations of enlightened buddhas.

If you have no established religion, you can still pick an archetype from one of the religions or from history to emulate, preferably one idealized by time whose baser human qualities have been forgotten, so that they serve as a model for the best of human qualities. If historians later discover that she beat her children, or he had sex with his slaves, just stick with the idealized archetype. We also will make mistakes and fail to conform to ideal thoughts, words, and deeds.

Persistence will improve our performance, however, and one day we may surprise ourselves by doing spontaneous acts of kindness. Cultivate that state of mind, and we may find our Hearts opening to others. Then we may find our Godhead within, and beyond all expectation, we may find an inexhaustible source of Love, inspiration, strength, and courage.

As always with Tantra, keep your realizations to yourself and trusted advisors. If you act like Christ in the world and shun accolades from others, you will probably be fine. But if you announce to the world that you are Jesus Christ returned and act like an asshole, you may be locked up. Act big, talk small.

THIS TECHNIQUE OVERCOMES PAIN in two ways. The first is that it makes you bigger than the pain. The second way is that it unlocks your inner healer.

LOOKING AT THE FIRST BENEFIT, as we find our Soul, we find a part of ourselves that is far stronger than the False Self that is our Ego. When we are in Ego mind, we are addicted to a certain level of pain. If we are addicted to all pleasure and no pain, our pleasure-seeking behavior, such as taking drugs, usually only defers pain until later, trapping us in an addiction cycle. If we are clinging to higher levels of pain because this has become the way we see ourselves, then the ways Ego seeks pain are usually harmful to the mind and body, eventually resulting in more pain than Ego bargained for. In either case, we get even more pain than Ego wanted, weakening Ego and eventually awakening the sleeping Soul.

For our Soul, pain cannot threaten its existence and can even strengthen it. So as our conscious awareness shifts (out of necessity) from our limited Ego to our awakening Soul, we find a strength beyond anything we could ever have imagined. The Soul can handle pain and grow from it. At the same time, the Soul does not need the pain and can (and will) let go of pain if it is being artificially maintained by Ego. Divine Soul connected with Ultimate Reality is not addicted to anything, which is why various twelve-step programs that connect the addict with God work the way they do.

In addition to weakening the Ego, a benefit of pain is expanding the range of pain and pleasure that we can tolerate. Few people seek pain. Pleasure is much more fun, but Ego has a fun limit as well as a pain limit. Because Ego is our habitual way of dealing with the world, Ego has a narrow range from pleasure to pain that is familiar. Just as Ego has an upper limit of pain that it finds familiar, so also does it have an upper limit to the level of pleasure that it feels comfortable with.

Pleasure is easy to stop just by ceasing the activity causing it, so we rarely exceed our Ego's pleasure limit. Pain is hard to stop, because we have little control over the outside forces that determine it. So a boxer may go into a fight to show how tough he is, that part is voluntary; but he has less control over how hard his opponent hits. We do not have control over how hard life hits us, so most of us grow beyond our Ego's narrow range of pleasure and pain by means of the pain we are unwillingly subjected to, not the pleasure which we can easily avoid. So a side benefit of withstanding great pain is growing our ability to withstand great pleasure. Because we know that great pain does not destroy us, we then also know that we can withstand more pleasure than humans who have not endured great pain.

This ability is a great benefit for Tantric practices that use pleasure to achieve transcendent states of being, and is especially useful for developing more capacity for pleasure during Tantric sex. Eventually you may even be able to endure the ecstasy of God's loving embrace, or however your religion or philosophy describes ecstatic union with all of Reality.

THE SECOND WAY THAT TANTRA overcomes pain is by unlocking our inner healer. The ability of meditation and prayer to heal is well documented. If this is just a placebo effect, who cares? The important part is to become healed. The Tantric view of this effect is that the Body possesses vast healing potential, and our Soul has a font of healing Energy that helps the Body achieve this healing potential.

However Ego only cares about maintaining itself and thinks of itself as the whole show. Ego sucks Life Energy from the Soul to maintain the Ego, which would evaporate like the fiction it is if Ego stopped drawing Energy. Ego hogs the Energy that would otherwise go to heal the Body. Remember that the kind of Life Energy that we are talking about here is not the ordinary energy of the Material world, but rather the Divine Energy of consciousness, which feels like attention to the Ego. Ego wants Soul and other people to pay attention to it. It is said that Energy flows where attention goes.

This is why Ego will drive people to commit horrible acts that make the news. Everyone then pays attention, which feeds the Egos involved. Egos thrive on drama because drama draws our attention. When we pay attention to crime and terrorism and other lurid events, our Energy flows to the participants, both the victims and the perpetrators. Especially the perpetrators. We are their enablers. In less dramatic form, we can see this effect in some flamboyant politicians. Performers can feel this Energy flow for themselves when their audience loves a great performance; in fact they often comment on the Energy of the audience.

A poorly adapted Ego that assumes command over our behavior will ignore signals from the Body that all is not well, and Ego will choose the wrong foods or the wrong quality of food, choose harmful drugs, or choose the wrong physical activity. Ego wreaks havoc on the Body with its defective life plans. When the Ego's plans fail to produce beneficial results, the brain and nervous system register negative psychological states that imbalance hormones and neurotransmitters, harming the Body if the imbalance is not corrected. As negative emotions arise from psychological and physical pain, the Ego is weakened, forcing Ego to draw even more Life Energy from the Soul to maintain itself. Subjectively, we pay attention to ourselves and blame outside forces for the problems created by our Egos. As attention focuses on our failing life plans and threatened self-concepts, Ego draws down the Life Energy which would otherwise be available to the Body to help heal itself, and physical and psychological problems become chronic, causing real long-term harm.

The Tantric solution for fixing this problem is to awaken the sleeping Soul and make the awareness of our Divine nature our primary consciousness. Soul will pull its Energy from an Ego life plan that is not working. This is annihilation for the False Self and is the reason why Ego will do *anything* to keep us from finding our Soul, our True Nature. Soul taking back its Life Energy supply frees up the Energy formerly used to maintain the Ego. This gives Soul extra Life Energy for other uses. Now with Life Energy to spare, paying attention to the pain of the Body allows this extra healing Energy to flow there, helping the Body heal.

Some cautions: Ego thinks it is your Soul and the whole world revolves around itself. Do not be fooled. The True Soul is selfless and will spontaneously help anything in pain, including the Body that carries it if it has the power to do so. Soul does not fear and does not suffer. You need to flush out Ego and pull its power cord, otherwise it will just find a new way to feed itself by pretending to be a healer. Be aware that if you remove the Ego's source of Energy, Ego will begin to die, and you will feel as if you are dying. This is because you have mistaken your False Self, Ego, for your True Self. Realize this and endure the death of the Ego, and you will find yourself free, with Energy to burn. This is mentally painful and takes time, but is worth it in the end. Just make sure you have taken that vow not to commit suicide in the section on Commitment, because Ego will even kill the Body to avoid destruction. Ego must surrender so that Soul can be free.

Other cautions: Do not expect healing energy to replace missing limbs, joints, or organs. Healing Energy can only work with what is there. Also, do not try using healing Energy exclusively. Modern medicine is very effective and there is no reason not to use it in concert with healing Energy and prayer. Science is discovering that healing is faster when all these are used together. Also, most medical professionals are motivated to heal others, so part of their effectiveness may be their ability to direct their healing Energy to you or to awaken your own healing Energy. Most medical professionals are unaware that they can do this, but there is a dawning awareness of what they call "therapeutic touch," and some are realizing that touch can speed recovery.

You may, however, have to restrain doctors who are control freaks or who think that they can improve the Body, which has been honed by millions of years of evolution. These are signs of Ego at work in your doctor. We are finding that medical procedures carry their own risks, in some cases higher risks than doing nothing. Make sure your doctor explains the risks versus the possible benefits and make your own decisions. Good doctors also realize you may be an expert on your own Body and its unique problems.

Summarizing turning Pain into the Path, pain can be beneficial by weakening the Ego (which is our enemy within), allowing Soul to become our primary consciousness. Pain benefits us by strengthening us and expanding our capacity to withstand transcendent pleasure. If we learn to withdraw our Soul's Life Energy from maintaining Ego and shift it to maintaining our Body, we unlock our inner healer. This the Tantric Way.

✂ WORK AS THE PATH: In Tantric practice, we are trying to turn our entire life into the Path to unite us with Reality. During our working years, we may spend most of our waking hours at work or thinking about work, which may be running a household, performing in one of the arts, or doing volunteer work, not necessarily paid work. How do we use this major portion of our lives to advance our spiritual practice?

The easy way is to choose an occupation that helps others and conduct yourself in an ethical manner while working. But if you work for something like a munitions manufacturer, there may be nothing ethical you can do, short of throwing shoes in the gears.

In this case the best action may be to do the best work you can do, and try to locate another job. But most jobs are neither totally beneficial nor totally harmful, and the way you conduct yourself determines if you are benefiting or harming others.

The Tantric method is to work selflessly and to visualize benefits flowing to others as a result of your work. So if you are working for a drug company, instead of concentrating on the money going to your paycheck and retirement plan, visualize healing Energy flowing into the products that will relieve pain or cure those who will be using the products. There are too many professions to be able to discuss how to apply Tantra to all of them. I will mention a few more examples to give you ideas for applying Tantra to your own work.

A particularly beneficial profession for the Tantric practitioner can be that of an actor. If one performs this job for the adoration of others, then being an actor can hold one back by feeding the Ego. However, if you do this job to entertain others and find joy in exploring different roles, both heroes and villains, then your motivation is generous and selfless, and you will be among the first humans to learn that our Egos, the roles we play to interact with others and our environment, are pure fiction. The ways we act in the world are but roles we play, not the actor who assumes that role. When a fan interacts with an actor as if the actor is a character the actor plays, then the actor can clearly see that the roles humans play are fiction, and we can change our roles by learning new ways to relate with our world. Our Ego, our persona, is not our True Self.

Let's take a harder example, soldiers in wartime. To some, this job supports the military-industrial complex, brings injury and death to others, and they believe this job is inherently harmful. To others, soldiers protect innocents from harm and liberate victims of oppression, and this job is inherently beneficial. The reality is, and Reality is what we are looking for, whether this job is beneficial or harmful depends on how soldiers conduct themselves.

So as a soldier, you enlisted to help others. You did not choose to put your life in danger and live in terrible conditions eating bad food for selfish reasons. If you had a touch of Ego desire to be seen as heroic or a badass—that got a quick reality check as soon as you found yourself under fire and realized that listening to your Ego could get you into total shit. Soldiers will stop listening to Ego.

Nowhere do you encounter reality in its rawest form than in wartime, and Reality is what shapes us. If the Universe is conscious and cares about people, here you will see it working through people. War is hell, but you will see angels at work. And soldiers are the first among us to discover that our enemies are just like us.

The soldier's ethics will be tested. Faced with an armed opponent, you may have to defend yourself, but faced with someone who is no threat to you, you may have to defy orders or resist peer pressure and let your Heart of compassion determine your actions. You will learn to restrain anger, accept risk to make good decisions, and forgive yourself for bad decisions. No one said life would be easy. For all life's work, if you pay attention, work will test you and grow you.

Warriors are found in all occupations. Not all Warriors kill. Broadly defined, a Warrior is one engaged in a struggle or conflict and is able to confront and overcome obstacles, useful traits on the Path of Ethics. To be a Warrior is to have a state of mind that accepts adversity to benefit others. In the West we regard Warriors highly, sometimes calling them "fighters," figuratively meaning someone who does not quit under duress.

The Path of the ethical Warrior can lead to victory and be beneficial to others, but has some pitfalls. One is the difficulty of ensuring the Warrior's cause is actually beneficial. Warriors are often exploited to fight for questionable causes by those in power. Warriors must consult their own Hearts of Love and not trust in the motivations of others, even those with worldly or spiritual credentials. Leaders may be driven by money or power. How do you tell ethical from non-ethical actions? Only when your mind is calm and centered in your Heart of Love.

Another pitfall is that viewing oneself as a Warrior may feed the Warrior's Ego. The mindset of the fighter is often very effective in dealing with the world and more likely to lead to victory over difficulties. This may strengthen the Ego structure, which makes yielding to a greater power difficult. So if you are a Warrior and have often prevailed, be sure you are always ready to surrender to superior forces, which on the Tantric Path means the forces of Love wielded by a Universe that cares about us. Like a good soldier who knows when the battle is over, and it is time to lay down arms, the true Warrior knows when to surrender.

✂ RAISING CHILDREN AS THE PATH: Almost any living creature, even animals and plants, can have sex and produce offspring. If that is the only part you play in raising children, you are no better than the weeds growing beside a path and the bugs that infest them.

Children are humans who have not yet reached their final adult form, often needy, selfish creatures requiring development from infant to child to adult, including many older adults. The term Children refers to a level of maturity, and many adults have not yet reached full maturity. To some extent, we are all Children here on Earth, meaning that most of us are not fully ready to make the world a better place. If the Mystics are correct, we are the

Children of God, the sentient Universe that cares about us. Capitalized, Children refers to this broader use of the term, as humans not yet fully mature, regardless of age.

The humans who help develop Children from what they are to adulthood come in at least three flavors: Parents, Teachers, and Coaches. Parents are humans that take on the responsibility to support a child from some stage of infancy, childhood, or young adulthood, providing food and shelter, discipline, and guidance in how to behave as humans. True Parenting has nothing to do with biological reproduction. Many Parents are also biological parents, but even these Parents realize that having sex and giving birth were the easy parts.

Teachers provide the functions and skills humans need to think for themselves and manage their lives. Teaching and Parenting functions overlap, and some Teachers also guide in how to behave and may even provide food and shelter for some.

Coaches tend to teach how to perform and excel at specific activities, often how to coordinate with other humans as part of a team. Coaching also overlaps with Parenting and Teaching, often providing role models, and health and fitness guidance. Some Coaches even feed and house their developing humans. Other Coaches are mentors for full adults, even seniors.

Good Parents, Teachers, and Coaches all share the same characteristics, regardless of the level of maturity of the Children they are working with. All three types act as role models, often mother figures and father figures. If a child's biological parents were defective, Teachers and Coaches can become mother and father figures for a developing human. Good Parents can make up for bad Teachers and poor Coaches. That is one of the ways Children with defective role models can still turn out okay. It takes a village to raise a child.

Raising, teaching, and coaching Children all require certain characteristics in order to be effective. The first of these is that the Parent, Teacher, or Coach must care. This cannot be faked. Children know. It is possible to begin these roles without caring, but if caring is absent, the Tantric way is to imagine and act as if you care. Over time, your inner state will align to match your outer state, and you will learn to care. If you care long enough, one day a child will touch your Heart and your Heart will begin to open, putting you into contact with the Universe, because your Divine Heart is part of that Universe. That is a Tantric goal.

A second characteristic is that you must know more or be more skilled or developed in the subject area than those you raise or teach. Duh. Mentors tell us that the quickest way to become well versed in a subject is to teach it. So Parenting can be a crash course in maturity for those who are helping Children mature. One of the best ways to become expert in a subject is to challenge yourself by teaching it, because your students will quickly uncover gaps in your knowledge and force you as Teacher to fill these gaps. Athletes may be skilled but often do not know to how they came by their skills or how to improve them. Coaches must delve their own depths and uncover the source of their own skills in order to assist others. Helping others in these ways are aspects of the Path of Ethics.

A third characteristic of those who would raise Children is patience. We see what happens when we lose patience with Children. Children can be advanced only so fast; experience teaches us how fast and the patience to accept this pace. Children cannot handle erratic behavior from their role models, which would destroy trust and the teaching relationship. Uncontrolled emotions can cause Children to dissolve into emotional chaos, and we learn from this to control our own emotions and behaviors. Buddhists call this mind control, which is an important aspect of the Tantric Path.

A fourth characteristic: We who develop Children must learn to balance praise and criticism. Give excess praise and Children fail to learn what life is like. Adults do not expect every effort to be rewarded, as well we should not. Life is stingy with rewards, and from this we learn persistence. However, reasonably correct behavior should receive praise, not criticism because behavior is less than perfect. Humans want approval for steps in the right direction and must not be made to require perfection to receive this approval. Excessive criticism and punishment crushes the spirit of Children and teaches them that they are inferior and can never please adults. Life is also not like this. We want praise for improvement and appropriate criticism for failures, coupled with advice for improvement. And praise must always exceed criticism. If you have not praised a child or developing adult recently, you may not criticize them until you have found something to compliment them for. You have lost your license to criticize. We are trying to teach Reality, and Reality calls for balance.

Excessive control also damages Children. We learn from our mistakes much faster than from our successes. Successes only reinforce our life plans, our Egos. We must not fear to allow children and developing adults to fail. Failure forces us to think about what went wrong and gives us the incentive to find answers. Parents, teachers, and coaches protect and guide learners from disastrous mistakes that would have permanently damaging consequences. But as much as possible, we should allow children and developing adults to learn for themselves what does not work. How can we know our limitations if we are not allowed to test them? How can developing humans learn to run their own lives if they are always managed and controlled by adults? They will grow up passive, expecting others to tell them what to do. The Western Tantric Way is to discover things for yourself, not blindly follow the instructions of others.

As we learn how to raise, teach, and coach Children, we learn how humans learn and grow, and that helps us realize how contact with Reality shapes us, even as adults. If we can become good Parents, Teachers, and Coaches, we may begin to see those same qualities in the way the Universe handles our own development, and this has the potential to develop our confidence that the Universe cares about us, so that we may let it shape us with less resistance. This can speed our progress on the Tantric Path.

⚸ COOKING AS THE PATH: The Energy that powers the Soul feels like Love and may be Love. Our first experience of Love is being fed by our mothers. As we develop, food is available in many flavors, and it is supplied by our parents with Love. Just as food is the energy that powers the Body, so also there may be a parallel or correlation between the ordinary energy that feeds our Bodies and the Life Energy that feeds our Souls. Both feel like Love to us. At least we can visualize food as Love. When we prepare food and feed others, we can visualize giving food as a tangible act of Love. This helps us to Love people in other ways.

Food, like Love, is available in many flavors. When preparing and serving food with Love, imagine the food you are making is food for the Soul. Soul food. As you prepare food to delight those who eat it, visualize adding flavors of Love to the food, flavors of friendship, and wishes that it will bring pleasure, satisfaction, sustenance, and health. People may actually experience your Love by means of your cooking.

When you eat the food you prepare, also give Love to the living plants and animals that gave up their Material lives to feed your Body and sustain the life you are using to become a better person and help others. Wish that their Spirit and Divine aspects feel your gratitude. Above all, do not treat their gift with distain by wasting it. Do not overeat or prepare excess food that you will have discard. When spilled or spoiled food must be discarded, think you are now feeding the small creatures, the bugs, worms, and bacteria whose lives will be sustained by what you do not consume. This builds awareness of Reality and our role in the Universe.

✄ RECREATION AS THE PATH: Recreation is an interesting word, to create again, like creating ourselves anew. Essentially when you relax and do something fun, you re-create yourself. You get back in touch with what makes up your deeper self and restore your health. Because we are trying to get in touch with Ultimate Reality and reality is all around us, technically anything you do can be turned into the Path if you pay attention to what you are doing.

But some activities are more fun to do and are more likely to command your full attention. The easiest ways to get into full contact with Reality are activities that are continuous and those that require skill and concentration. Some examples include surfing, skiing, running, driving, sailing, golf, fishing, and archery. Even better are activities requiring coordination with other people, such as dancing, singing in a group, playing in a band or orchestra, and sports requiring continuous, coordinated teamwork.

To use recreation to fully contact Reality, first become so skilled that you can do the activity without thinking about what you are doing. Thinking is the enemy of discovering Reality, because the brain processing time needed to analyze sensory inputs and formulate body responses puts us fractions of a second behind present reality. We are playing catch-up, reacting not to the present but to what happened moments ago with a small time-lag. So the thinking dancer is thinking about which foot to move and what move to try next and how not to bump into other dancers. The skilled dancer does not need to think about how to do the steps and is free to synchronize her body movements with her partner and can go with the flow of the music, becoming part of the dynamic whole.

To go with the flow you must let yourself go. Stop thinking and be in the moment. Become one with the music or the river or the wave or the road. Become one with the chorus or the team or the crowd. Drop all boundaries between yourself and your surroundings. When you fully synchronize with reality you will feel a rush, a moment of ecstasy, a taste of eternity. These are "Wow Moments," moments to cherish and try to experience again. Every time you synchronize with a dynamic Totality, your Soul awakens a bit more. It grows, never to un-grow.

In time with repetition, you may even experience what the Mystics call God. Let's restore ourselves to the mind of a child, the mind that can experience awe as if seeing something for the first time. This is another Tantric technique for using pleasure as the Path. Have fun here; someday we will have to leave.

✄ DYING AS THE PATH: Experiencing the full extent of life eventually brings us to the process of dying. As with all of life's activities, it is wise to be able to do this last act of our present life well. Most of us think of death as "bad," a punishment or some sort of failure to live longer. Logically, this is wrong. If we are immortal Souls and will meet God at the death of our Bodies, then death is nothing but a change of state. If we are only mortal, death will just be a natural consequence of life, for many a relief from life's stresses.

One could argue that the sooner and easier the death, the better. Certainly death cannot be a punishment for the one who dies if it happens to everyone, regardless of their virtues. Death could only be considered a punishment for those who benefited from the deceased, never for the one who died. Maybe the manner of death can be considered a punishment, if only briefly, in which case the most fortunate people on Earth are those executed quickly and humanely, and the least fortunate are those who live long with painful illnesses or guilt from wrongdoing or loss of freedom. So the death penalty punishes the friends and family of the one executed and rewards the one executed with a painless early release from a life of guilt and imprisonment. Clearly there are inconsistencies with the conventional Western views of death and punishment.

However, that is not the Tantric view of life and death. In Tantra, life is almost always beneficial, regardless of the circumstances. Why? Because in every moment we are relating to Reality, and if we pay attention and do not resist life's lessons, we learn from Reality and evolve. Ego has its plans and hopes for us, but reality is what actually happens. In the Tantric view, consciousness continues beyond death which is just a transition from one life to the next. The consciousness that continues we call our Divine Formless Soul, and because Soul knows that life continues, our Soul does not fear death. In fact, for some of us it is an adventure, and for all of us it is an opportunity for change.

Fear of death is almost universal, but the part of us that fears is Ego, our personality and plan for dealing with our current life. The transition of death is change. The risk to Ego is that our roles and plans for interacting with our current life may not work during the death transition or the life after death. The current Ego may have to dissolve so that a new plan can be created for dealing with the new life. In other words, Ego is threatened with annihilation with every major life change, even changes that the Body survives. Ego is the part of us that fears.

The greatest change that any of us can face is acceptance of Ultimate Reality, poetically, the Soul's union with God, the created joining with the Creator, Subtle Mind uniting with Emptiness, our deepest wish. There is no place for Ego's separate self in this union with the Universe. Ego's limited plan and role must dissolve if we are to experience our true purpose and identity. Our conventional view of ourselves must die so that we can be born again to our true nature, empty of limitations and interrelated with all that exists.

The potential to become one with the Universe exists with every change in our life and with the changes inherent in death. Our Heart longs for this union, which accounts for our persistent feelings that something really important is missing from our lives. But our concept of a separate unchanging self, our Ego, is terrified of letting go and will do everything in its power to stop the Soul from learning that we are not our limited role and purpose. Expect to be distracted at every turn by ordinary cares that prevent you from finding and liberating your Soul. Keep up your spiritual practices in the face of opposition, and Ego must eventually surrender to Reality and you will be free, both in life and the life after death.

*"As I wander through the dark, encountering difficulties,
I am aware of encouraging voices that murmur from the
spirit realm. I sense a holy passion pouring down from
the springs of Infinity. I thrill to the music that beats
with the pulses of God. Bound to suns and planets by
invisible cords, I feel the flames of eternity in my soul.
Here, in the midst of the every-day air, I sense the rush of
ethereal rains. I am conscious of the splendour that binds
all things of earth to all things of heaven—immured by*

silence and darkness, I possess the light which shall give
me vision a thousandfold when death sets me free."
—Hellen Keller, *My Religion*

We usually do not know the exact moment or manner of our death, so it is best to prepare ourselves to face this change while we are strong and healthy. Preparing for death will not make it happen sooner. Conventionally, it is important to have final instructions which symbolically detach you from material possessions that you cannot take with you. Trying to grasp at material things as they slip away will only cause distress. Resolve problems with people as they occur, or forgive and forget issues that are not worth fighting over. Carrying a grudge or a wish for reconciliation on your death-bed will distract you from the work at hand.

From a Tantric view, death is an adventure and an opportunity for liberation from ordinary life. What you see during the dying process is thought to be a series of symbolic representations of an underlying invisible reality, and the visions are created by your our own mind, so the reported experiences of those who have nearly or briefly died differ, depending on the person and their state of mind. Some may have a vision of trusted figures sent to guide them, and they go with their guides. Some see lights, and the courageous choose the greatest source of light and Love over the lesser and familiar lights. Others see darkness turn into the clear light of a cloudless day and relax and try to remain in the clear light as long as possible. Still others see their life and life purpose, and are offered a choice to return to that life or to move on. To be honest, some see hellish visions, but report it is never too late to repent and pray for help. Whatever the vision, most agree that it is best to relax and let go as each vision presents itself.

THE TANTRIC VIEW IS THAT heaven and hell are not places but instead are states of mind determined by the benefits and harm to others we inflict during our life. Because these are states of mind, neither heaven nor hell is forever. We can pay off Karmic debts and cure a hellish state of mind or leave a heavenly state of mind to help people in distress. Because we tend to carry the same state of mind that we had in this life to our next life, it is best to find heaven while we still live. Here in a human life, we can learn from others who have found the Way to a heavenly state of mind or a heavenly place of being.

Eastern Buddhist concepts of what Westerners call heaven are virtual locations in one of the Form realms, where an enlightened spiritual master such as Christ or Buddha has created an ideal space for learning. In these places of learning, those with the Karma to be there can learn to train their minds, free from the Material distractions such as: poor seating and lighting, hunger, thirst, illness, having to pee or crap, cold or heat, dirt, weather, bugs, poor acoustics, language barriers, discriminatory laws, and the many other distractions of the Material world that degrade the learning experience. Imagine that your favorite enlightened masters could create the perfect learning environments, and that you could be in their presence to learn directly from them. In the Tantric view, this is possible.

> "I must go down to the seas again, to the lonely sea and sky,
> and all I ask is a tall ship and a star to steer her by. . . ."
> —John Masefield, Sea Fever

HAVING PREPARED IN ADVANCE FOR your own death by cultivating a heavenly state of mind as best you can while living, what do the wise say to do when it is clear that you are actually dying?

Obviously, you have to memorize these instructions in preparation for this moment, because there is no time to cram for this exam as you are dying. As your Material aspects disintegrate, such as the ability to move your muscles, you will have a choice to either fight the loss of each dissolution of your Material aspects or let go. Clinging and fighting the loss of the dying Material Body's functions is futile and will bring failure and terror at not being able to stop the process of dying. The correct thought and response as each Material aspect dissolves is to let go and let it happen. Let go, let go, let go, let go. . . .

Eventually your vision will be of utter darkness, and if you can think, think that this darkness is merely the darkness before the dawn of a new life. Let go and wait patiently, and you will see a clear light as of a new dawn on a cloudless day, as clear as the sky after a rain. The clear light may be white or of many colors that combine to appear white. Remain in this clear light as long as possible. Your ability to remain in the clear light will depend on how well you trained your mind to be still during your human life. If a small object appears in your field of vision, rest your attention peacefully on this small object as long as possible, and your Divine nature will blossom. After the clear light experience, the former visions may return in reverse order, and you find yourself between lives.

Based on Buddhist texts and reports from those with death and near-death experiences, here between lives you choose your next life. What you see here depends on the state of your mind, and on the Karma you generated during your human life. Hopefully you developed a strong relationship with your Base religion or philosophy and will be guided to whatever next life is most beneficial for you. But if your visions are of a hellish nature, reflecting the state of your mind, realize that it is never too late to repent things you may have done in life and pray for assistance and aid. Many report seeing a review of their entire life, generally described as from others' points of view rather than their own.

Remember now that no one is perfect, and all of us could use more work. Do not condemn yourself for minor flaws. If offered choices of different lives, different realms, or different lights, do not panic and flee to the familiar, or worse, flee to wherever your Karma throws you. Stay calm, set your Heart compass to the greatest source of light and Love, and go where your Heart leads. If you need more work, you may find one of the perfect places of learning mentioned earlier. Hopefully your Heart compass will lead you to God or whatever you prefer calling the source of Love. When you arrive at the Source, there is where strong Tantric practice really pays off. Faced with overwhelming Love and ecstasy, will you bask in a lesser experience of Love from a distance and pass on to a lesser life for more training? Or will you have enough courage and experience gained on the Tantric Path to embrace the source of Love? That is the question. You are the answer.

"All that lives must die, passing through nature to eternity."
—William Shakespeare, *Hamlet*

HOMEWORK:

1. Look at the list of human adversity:

[ ] poverty	[ ] pain	[ ] alienation
[ ] hunger	[ ] disability	[ ] obscurity
[ ] unemployment	[ ] aging	[ ] insanity
[ ] homelessness	[ ] death	[ ] addiction
[ ] illness	[ ] loneliness	[ ] abuse

[ ] enslavement   [ ] torture   [ ] anger

[ ] discrimination   [ ] imprisonment   [ ] violence

[ ] persecution   [ ] fear   [ ] war

[ ] theft   [ ] hate

Check off the ones you have already experienced. From the list of those you have not yet experienced, pick one and find a way through charity organizations like The Red Cross, Goodwill, Salvation Army, soup kitchens, prison ministry, hospice or other sources to gain experience in that area. Then move to the next adversity. Record the results in your journal. If you have checked off all the adversities, say "No, no, Lord, I'm not ready to go yet. I need more work on [pick an adversity]" and work on that.

2. Watch the movie *The Revenant*, which is a true story. Say to yourself, "This is how tough my human body can be." Is your Ego this tough? If not, why not?

3. Watch the movie *Star Trek: the Motion Picture*. Observe how non-aggression and non-resistance lead to the center of the cloud of unknowing. Note how joining with the creator requires the union of male and female elements and that this joining leads to new life, the child's mind able to access the entire universe and other dimensions.

4. If you wish for more detailed instructions and practices for dying, consult with your Base spiritual practice. If you want the detailed Buddhist instructions, take a course in death and dying and read about the eight stages of dissolution.

FURTHER READING:

Adversity: At a very difficult period in my life, the only thing that helped me feel better was reading Lama Zopa Rinpoche's *Transforming Problems into Happiness*. I underlined the passages that were especially helpful to me, and reread the underlined parts every time I was in distress, which was almost daily. The book may have saved my life. If you are experiencing adversity, this book may also help you.

Dying: For more details and inspiring stories about death and dying, read *The Tibetan Book of Living* and Dying by Sogyal Rinpoche.

GOD WITH A
BROKEN WAND

A FAIRY TALE FOR CHILDREN

magine that you are God and your magic wand is broken. When
the wand was working, you filled the Earth with an abundance of
everything, and all the creatures had what they need because they
evolved to use what was there. Whatever the food and water and
atmosphere and temperature available in a particular place, they
became the creatures that needed that.

Then people evolved, and with their hands and brains they
changed the places where they were to suit themselves. They pros-
pered and filled the planet and started running out of things to
sustain themselves. Now there is still enough for all, but people
are not yet as intelligent or as loving as God, so some people have
surpluses, and others have shortages and are really hurting.

If your magic wand was working, you could create more stuff
out of nothing, as you did in the beginning, when there was only

a tiny singularity to start with. But the magic wand is broken, and you still love your creatures, and you want them to have what they need. You realize that all needs can still be met, but to do that, you now have to work through people to move things that are needed from where they are abundant to where they are scarce. Of all the creatures, only people have the power and intelligence to do that.

But fear makes that difficult. People who have things are afraid they will run out, so they keep more than they need. From the beginning, every creature has a bit of you in their heart, so you start working on those hearts to get them to move things from where they are to where they are needed, but you find most people's hearts are closed and nothing happens.

Remember, you are seeing yourself as God, and your magic wand is broken, and you have to work through people. Now what are you going to do? You do the only thing you can do: you watch people and see who shares what they have with those who are in need, and then use what influence you have over the hearts of people and the natural forces of nature to make sure resources flow to the people who will pass it on.

You see that some people keep all that they are given, and you ignore them because they are taking care of themselves. And you see that some people take everything from others, leaving victims without what they need; so you do what you can, working through the hearts of others to keep the takers away from the sharers. That is the best you can do without a magic wand; you work through people, ignoring the keepers, thwarting the takers, and making sure resources flow to the sharers who pass them on to those who need.

Now imagine that you are human and want to know if God exists. If there is a loving God, God must not have a magic wand;

otherwise there would be no one in need. If you are a keeper out of fear or greed and have more than you need, you can expect to be ignored by God, and in that way know that God exists. If you are a taker, you can expect to be thwarted by God, and in that way know that God exists. If you are in need, you can expect open-hearted people to help you, and in that way know that God exists. If you share what you do not need with those in need, then you can expect to see resources flow to you, so that you can pass them on, and in that way know that God exists.

Now imagine you are the hands of God in the world, and God's magic wand is broken. Of the choices of how to be—greedy, needy, taker, or sharer—I think the generous person, the sharer, will have the more interesting life. If you see someone in need, you will see a way to help them. If you receive a windfall, watch and the people who need it will appear. Of the ways to be, which will *you* choose?

GLOSSARY

Note that a few key terms in lower case are included. Western Tantra uses these words in the same way as certain spiritual traditions commonly use these terms, but these terms may not be clear to all readers.

Addiction: The inability to limit the use of a substance or behavior, including excessive food, alcohol, drugs, sex, work, gambling, electronic games, social media, and many other things to the extent that the use is harmful to oneself or others. The modern term for the outdated term Gluttony, one of the West's "seven deadly sins."

All: See God.

angel: The Western term for a sentient being whose Heart is in communication with the Divine, and who is able to appear in the Material or Spirit realm to benefit others using what skills and resources the angel has available, similar to the Buddhist term bodhisattva (awakening being) and the Western term saint. Angels may or may not be Enlightened. Enlightened angels are the same as buddhas.

Apparition: See Ego.

Back: See Past.

Base: When referring to religion or philosophy, this is one's core religion or philosophy, often the religion one was born with or committed to in some way.

Between: See Spirit.

Beyond: See Divine.

bodhisattva: The Buddhist term bodhisattva means "awakening being." Bodhisattvas care for all sentient beings and appear in the Material and Spirit realms to help others. This term is similar to the Western terms angel and saint. Enlightened bodhisattvas are the same as buddhas.

Body: A physical human Body in the Material realm made up of ordinary matter and energy. The Body has a mostly fixed form and is mortal, having a finite lifespan. The thinking organs for the Body are the brain and nervous system, referred to as the Head.

Body-Mind: A thinking organ called the brain located in the skull. Synonym: Head.

Breath: See Energy.

buddha: The Buddhist term meaning "awake" designating an Enlightened being of the Divine realm who is able to appear in the Material or Spirit realm at will, has an aspect in all three realms, and who benefits others in the ways that are most beneficial for all concerned.

Bullet-Time: As seen in the movie *The Matrix*, Bullet-Time is experiencing reality with the faster speed of the Soul rather than the normal speed of the human nervous system, making events appear to happen in slow motion.

Cause and Effect: See Karma.

chakra: An Energy distribution center of the Spirit Body.

Chi: See Energy.

Children: Children are humans who have not yet reached their final adult form, often needy, selfish creatures needing development from infant to child to young adult, including many full-grown adults. The term Children refers to a level of maturity, and many adults have not yet reached full maturity. Capitalized, Children refers to the broader use of the term as humans not yet fully mature, regardless of age.

Coaches: Coaches teach humans how to perform and excel at specific activities, often how to coordinate with other humans as part of a team. Functions may overlap with those of Parents and Teachers.

Commitment: A promise to persist with Path practices for a lifetime.

Concept: See Spirit.

consciousness: Our sense of awareness. Its nature and origin is currently unknown, but may be a fundamental property of the information that defines physical systems, including spin, charge, and mass.

Dark, Darkness: Aspects of the universe that science has so far been unable to explain. Synonyms: Hidden, Unseen.

Divine: The Divine or Formless is the invisible and formless realm that pervades all realms of existence. Buddhists call this Emptiness, meaning empty of fixed inherent existence. The Divine or Formless is Pure Potential, anything that could exist. All things manifest arise from the Divine and eventually return

to the Divine. The unwritten laws of the universe which determine all reality are placed here. The Observer, our Soul, lives here
as does Love, joy, and awe. God concepts described as nameless,
secret, and unknowable belong here. Consciousness rules here.
Synonyms: Formless, Eternal, Ultimate, Un-manifest, Ineffable,
Transcendent, Beyond the Beyond, Unknowing, Emptiness, Fullness, Infinity, Ground-State, Pure Potential, Pure Awareness.

Dream: See Spirit.

Ecstasy: Ecstasy is a transcendent state of being in which the
False Self or Ego and even the entire Material world disappear
momentarily, silencing discursive mind.

Ego: Our life plan for interacting with our environment which
includes: our mental images of ourselves which more or less
correspond to the way we look physically, and the way others tell
us we look and act, and the ways we typically relate to the world.
This set of Form images exists in the realm of thought, the Spirit
realm. Because the Ego is a mental concept with no Physical reality, it does not necessarily die with the body. If adopted and fed
by the immortal Soul, Ego can be carried to the next life. Synonyms for our human Ego as the term is used here include False
Self, Personality, Spirit, Apparition, and Ghost.

Ego Mind: The thinking functions of the Ego, our habitual ways
of thinking. Ego Mind is a mental construct with a point of view
or focus of attention. If Ego Mind does not have its own thinking
functions it may just focus its attention on the Body's brain for
rational thought or the Soul's Heart for intuition. Ego Mind can
be changed and trained to be still. Synonym: Selfish Mind

Emptiness: See Divine and God.

Energy: When capitalized, Energy means a source of conscious-ness energy called Prana, Inner Fire, Chi, Qi, Ki, Kundalini, Power, Mana, Medicine, Juju, Life Force, Breath, Light, and other names. Many spiritual systems divide this energy into two flavors, often called male and female energy. This Energy feels like Love and may be Love, but we will mainly call it Energy or Life Force. This Energy is not the ordinary energy which has a matter equivalence.

Enlightened/Enlightenment: Enlightened or Enlightenment refers to the Buddhist use of the term meaning a consciousness that has full access to the Divine realm, in fact complete access to all three realms. The Christian translation of this term is one who is in union with God.

Envy: Resentment for an advantage possessed by another person and wishing to have what they have. A type of mental theft. One of the West's "seven deadly sins."

Eternal: See Divine.

Ethical: Ethical refers to actions that are intended to benefit others, or at least benefit the most with the least harm to the fewest number.

Experts: Experts are those with special skills or knowledge who have usually spent over ten thousand hours of training, over five years of full-time study, to be able to do what they do. Over twenty thousand hours would be more typical. For some, it is a lifetime of work.

Fact: Something generally accepted as accurate from a particu-lar point of view, relative to the user. The opposites of Fact are Fiction and Lies. This differs from the conventional definition which assumes facts are independently and inherently accurate for everyone. It is a mistake to try to impose your Facts on another person living a different reality from yours.

False Self: See Ego.

False: Frequently used in Eastern Tantric texts, false as used both here and in *Webster's* is something that appears to be true but is not. The important thing to note is that false things appear to be true, as opposed to things that are just plain wrong. Synonym: Illusory.

Fantasy: See Spirit.

Fighter: Used here figuratively, it means someone who does not quit under duress.

Form: Form means having some sort of manifestation, either physical or mental. Physical Forms include visible and touchable things, sounds, smells, and energy that can be sensed with the ordinary bodily senses and with scientific instruments. These are things made of ordinary matter or energy that make up the Material world. Mental Forms are thoughts and concepts that can imagined in the mind, including mental representations of words, numbers, symbols, sounds, smells, ideas, images, visions, concepts, and anything else that can be represented in our minds. These are made of thought, not matter or ordinary energy, but can be sensed in the "mind's eye." There are two Form realms of exis-tence: The Material world made of physical Forms and the Spirit world, made of Mental Forms. A synonym for Form is Manifest.

Formless: See Divine.

Free Will: Free Will is our ability to affect the Present.

Fullness: See Divine and God.

Future: This aspect of time is what is affected by what happens in the Present. At any given moment of time, the Future only exists as a set of probabilities for what may happen. By our actions in the Present, we can affect what Future probabilities become the next Present moment. Synonym: Next.

Ghost: See Ego and Spirit.

Gluttony: See Addiction.

God: As used here, God is defined as the entire universe or multiverse encompassing everything: all that ever existed, exists now, or ever could exist, both seen and unseen, Form and Formless. Synonyms for God: Universe, Ultimate, Reality, Totality, All, Infinity, Emptiness, Fullness, Allah, Yahweh, others.

Godhead: See Soul.

Greed: Taking for oneself more resources than one needs or more than one's fair share. One of the West's "seven deadly sins."

Ground-State: See Divine.

Guru, Guide: In the Eastern Tantras an experienced and trustworthy spiritual advisor who is well familiar with the scriptures and practices providing access to the Divine realm.

hate: A form of sustained anger. Hostility or aversion arising from anger, fear, or perceived injury.

Head: The brain and nervous system of the physical Body. Body sensory organs gather information from the outside world in the form of nerve impulses which are sent to the brain where they can be processed or stored as needed. Discursive thought and reasoning take place in the Head. The Head is capable of thought using mental constructs called words, numbers, symbols, and images which represent aspects of outer reality derived from stored sensory information that we call memory. Synonym: Body-Mind.

Heart/ Heart-Mind: The sentient aspect of the Soul, the seat of consciousness or Subtle Mind. Heart thoughts are no-thought, intuition, doing without thinking, instant knowing. Instant knowing is like a burst transmission, containing compressed meaning which can be instantly available or can be unpacked to play out over time in the realm of thought as emotions, poetry, art, music and dreams. Synonyms: Intuitive Mind, Subtle Mind.

heaven: A peaceful state of mind characterized by mental stability, happiness, and Love. As places, heavens are peaceful regions created by Loving or Enlightened minds which are conducive to learning the Path to Enlightenment. The term is not capitalized because its use here is similar to common usage. Synonym: Pure Land.

hell: A state of mind characterized by lack of control, suffering, disorder, harmful emotions, and wishing harm to others. As places, hells are regions inhabited by suffering beings who harm each other and where learning the Way to Enlightenment is made difficult. Beings can leave hells by changing their state of mind. The term is not capitalized because its use here is similar to common usage.

History: See Past.

Honor: As used here, Honor means to make your word your bond and make your actions match your words, as in "We Honor our commitments."

I: The focus of each person's attention or concentration is our "I, me, or my" point of view. Its location is usually in the Head attending to the sensory information from the Body and one's thoughts. Our focus of attention is very mobile and can be almost anywhere. When our focus of attention is our Heart, the seat of consciousness, we have access to intuition. The "I" is who we say we are, as in "I am" this or that. Most people use "I" to designate their Ego, but those who identify with Soul and have become selfless still have to use the words "I, me, and my" to refer to themselves when inhabiting a human body.

Illusory: See False.

Imaginary: See Spirit.

Ineffable: See Divine.

Infinity: See Divine and God.

information: Information in general is that which reduces uncertainty (entropy). Physical information is the information such as spin, charge, and mass which defines physical systems, such as particles and fields. The fundamental physical information defining a system cannot be destroyed. This is conservation of information, currently a law of physics.

Inner Fire: See Energy. This term also refers to the Energy which powers the Spirit Body described in the section on Tantric Sex. Inner Fire can be generated by the advanced Buddhist practice called Tummo, which requires Buddhist commitments and initiation.

Integrity: As used here, Integrity means to make your thoughts match your words and actions, worthy of trust, honest.

Interpenetration: During sexual practices, this refers to the penetration of both partners by the other with Divine Energy. Both genders are capable of doing this.

In-The-Moment: See Present.

Intuitive Mind: See Heart.

Journey: See Path.

Juju: See Energy.

Karma: This is the relationship between effects and their causes. For we who live in Linear Time, a cause is something which precedes and determines an effect. In the Present moment, we are experiencing effects determined by causes which occurred in the Past, and our actions in the Present are causes which become effects in the Future. Karma can also refer to the effects that have occurred or will occur as a result of our prior thoughts, words, or deeds. Karma is often described as positive or negative based on whether our actions were intended to benefit or harm others. Synonym: Cause and Effect.

Ki: See Energy.

Laziness: Failing to realize that our human life has a duration, and if we want our life to have meaning, then we do not have time to waste. One of the West's "seven deadly sins." Synonym: Sloth.

Life Force: See Energy.

Light: See Energy.

Linear Time: Time which progresses from Past to Present to Future with no branches. This is the time we ordinary human beings perceive, but this may not be universal.

Love: When capitalized here, Love means universal unconditional love or the Energy and power of unconditional love for all. Love for all with no conditions whatsoever. This is the Love between God and humanity. What naturally follows from Love is the wish to provide all living beings with pleasure and to remove pain from all beings who are suffering, which we call compassion. Love is the principal practice of Western Tantra.

Lust: Sex for personal pleasure, Plan A. Lust is one of the West's "seven deadly sins."

Mana: See Energy.

Manifest: See Form.

Material: The realm we ordinarily experience is the Material or Physical realm or world, the physical universe made up of ordinary matter and energy that we can experience with our body senses, and science can measure with instruments. This is one of the two Form realms. Synonyms: Physical, Real, Visible.

Medicine: See Energy.

Mental Form: See Spirit.

Mindfulness: A type of meditation in which one pays full attention to whatever one is doing at all times.

Miracle: A Miracle is a natural occurrence that is either so rare or so improbable in its timing and beneficial in its outcome that it suggests the presence of Divine intervention.

Mystic, Mystical: The Mystic is one who has a direct link to the Divine realm or to the Spirit world acting as an intermediary to the Divine realm. The Mystic gets instructions and knowledge directly from Ultimate Reality rather than scriptures. Mystical means that which is in direct contact with Ultimate Reality. As used here, Mystic and Mystical do not refer to occult or "dark magic" practices in any way.

Next: See Future.

No-Self: See Soul.

Now: See Present.

Observer, The: See Soul.

Occam's razor: A philosophical and scientific principle stating that among competing theories, the one with the fewest assumptions should be selected as the one most likely to be true.

Parents: Parents are humans that take on the responsibility to support a child from some stage of infancy, childhood, or young adulthood, providing food and shelter and discipline and guidance in how to behave as humans. As used here capitalized, True Parenting has nothing to do with biological reproduction.

Past: The past is something that already happened and cannot be changed, relative to our particular location, velocity and acceleration. The Past is what we use to predict the Future. Synonyms for the Past: History, Then, Back.

Path of Ethics: The Path of Ethics is the Western Tantric spiritual Path characterized by ethical action in the material world. Action means doing something tangible and visible. Ethical action is action which is intended to benefit others or at least benefit most people with the least harm to the fewest number.

Path: Used in its capitalized form here, the term Path refers to a set of techniques to reach Ultimate Reality. Spiritual Paths are *always* meant figuratively as a recipe or steps to achieve spiritual realizations. Synonyms for Path include Way, Journey, Road, and Vehicle.

persona: The social façade an individual assumes or the character in a book or play.

Personality: See Ego.

Physical: See Material.

Power: See Energy.

Prana: See Energy.

Present: The currently active moment of time, based on our particular location in space-time. This is the only moment when reality is fluid and we can change what is happening. From our perspective, only the Present moment exists. Synonyms: Now, In-The-Moment.

Pride: A mental state of mind which exalts one's personal attributes, achievements, or possessions used by Ego to protect itself from change. It is one of the West's "seven deadly sins."

Pure Awareness: See Divine.

Pure Land: See heaven as places.

Pure Potential: See Divine.

Qi: See Energy.

Real: See Material.

Reality: See God.

Renunciation: Rejection of the Material world and physical possessions as solutions for most problems. The mental state of one who looks to the Spirit and Divine for the pathways to the eternal.

Road: See Path.

Scientific Method: The systematic and objective process used by Western science to formulate and test theories about the laws governing the universe and extend human knowledge of how things exist and function.

sentient: Consciously aware and able to process and respond to the senses; the ability to do mental work. It may be a measure of how well information (consciousness) is integrated.

Sin: A bad translation from an original Hebrew archery term which meant "to miss the mark," to fail to hit the center of the target one is aiming for. Used here, sin means that some of our actions fall short of what a sentient Universe would like from us. We missed the point, we failed to hit the center of the target God set for us.

Sloth: See Laziness.

Soul: Soul refers to our deepest ultimate nature or aspect, pure consciousness dwelling in the Formless realm, our Divine nature, our pearl of great price, the pure light hidden within each of us, our ground state of being, the godhead within. Soul is Formless and without boundaries. Soul outlives the Body and may be immortal. Our Soul seems to be centered in the Body near the physical heart and may extend beyond the Body. Synonyms used here for Soul are True Self, True Nature, No-Self, Godhead, The Observer, Subtle Consciousness or Subtle Mind.

Spirit: Spirit is the realm of words, ideas, concepts, thoughts, images, projections, states of mind, dreams and visions including visualized forms as products of consciousness, Mental Forms. Pure lands, heavens, and hells are here. Religions which assign their highest supreme beings definite form and characteristics place them in this realm by definition. The concepts of Ego and Self live here. Synonyms: Thought, Imaginary, Fantasy, Word, Concept, Ghost, Dream, Between, Beyond, Bardo, Mental Form.

Spirit Body: A visualized structure which distributes Spirit Energy throughout the Body. The Spirit Body or "diamond" body is thought to have a hollow central channel from the top of the head to the floor of the pelvis. The central channel is flanked by two thinner channels, said to convey male and female Energy to an Energy center at the navel, where male and female Energy combine to power the Spirit Body. Energy distribution centers called chakras are spaced along the central channel.

Subtle Consciousness: See Soul.

Subtle Mind: See Soul.

Tantra/Tantric: The methods of spiritual transformation described in this book. These include visualizing ourselves and acting at all times as if we have actually achieved the ultimate goal any person can reach and harnessing the power of our emotions to drive our vision of our transformation.

Teachers: Teachers provide the functions and skills humans need to think for themselves and manage their lives. Teaching and Parenting functions overlap and some Teachers also guide how to behave and may even provide food and shelter for some.

Then: See Past.

Thought: See Spirit.

Three Times, The: The three elements of Time: Past, Present, and Future.

Time: Time is a dimension of the Universe which is used to express the duration of existence and rate of change. For us, Time is an arrow that points and moves only to the Future, although physics says time is flexible and may be reversible.

Tool: A Tool refers to a single technique or method that will help achieve a particular objective as part of the Western Tantric Path.

Totality: See God.

Transcendent: See Divine.

True Nature: See Soul.

True Self: See Soul.

True: Often used incorrectly in Eastern Tantric texts, both here and in *Webster's*, True and Truth will designate something that is correct, real, and can be relied on.

Ultimate: See Divine and God.

Universe: See God.

Unknowing: See Divine.

Un-manifest: See Divine.

Vehicle: See Path.

Visible: See Material.

Warrior: Broadly defined, a Warrior is one engaged in a struggle or conflict who is able to confront and overcome obstacles. To be a Warrior is to have a state of mind that accepts adversity to benefit others. Similar in meaning to "fighters," figuratively meaning someone who does not quit under duress.

Way: See Path.

West, Western: The West is the collection of democratic, pluralistic countries of the developed west; occidental. Roughly, this means regions influenced by European cultures. Cultural belief systems of the Western world include democracy, individual and personal freedom, equality, human rights, the Abrahamic religions, capitalism, science and the scientific method, and public education.

Western Tantra/Tantric: Western Tantra as a specific practice is the universal aspect of the traditional forms of Tantra practiced in the Eastern religions, stripped of its Eastern cultural trappings and reframed and re-populated with the cultural foundations of the Western nations. When used in italics, *Western Tantra* refers to the title of this book. As used here, the term Western Tantra never refers to neotantra or its modern practices or occult practices.

White Path: The *Western Tantra White Path of Ethics*. In Buddhism, white symbolizes the crown energy center and skillful means or actions. The White Path of Ethics refers to the spiritual path that uses performing altruistic acts in the Real world to create positive Karma and the capacity for Universal Love.

Wisdom: Wisdom means understanding how Reality works, that nothing exists on its own, independent of the rest of the universe. All things are interdependent. Wisdom is a complete understanding of Emptiness and the Divine realm which pervade all things and from which all things manifest arise.

Word: See Spirit.

Wow Moments: Brief experiences of synchronizing with a dynamic Totality, resulting in an emotional rush, a moment of ecstasy, a taste of eternity. Losing oneself in the joy of the present moment. Experiencing wonder or awe.

Wrath: Anger or hate, especially extreme anger. One of the West's "seven deadly sins."

BIBLIOGRAPHY

Calder, Nigel. *Einstein's Universe.* New York: Penguin Books, 1980.

Campbell, Joseph. *The Hero with a Thousand Faces.* Novato, CA: New World Library, 1999.

Campbell, Joseph. *The Power of Myth.* New York: Anchor Books, 1991.

Chaisson, Eric J. *Cosmic Evolution.* Cambridge, MA: Harvard University Press, 2001.

Cousins, Ewart. *Bonaventure.* Mahwah, NJ: Paulist Press. 1968.

English, Elizabeth. *Vajrayogini, Her Visualizations, Rituals, and Forms.* Boston: Wisdom Publications, 1987.

Easwaran, Eknath. *Nonviolent Soldier of Islam.* Tomales, CA: Nilgiri Press, 1999.

Evans-Wentz, W. Y., editor. *The Tibetan Book of the Dead.* New York: Oxford University Press, 1960.

Genz, Henning. *Nothingness, the Science of Empty Space.* Cambridge, MA: Perseus Publishing, 1999.

Greene, Brian. *The Elegant Universe.* New York: Vintage Books, 2003.

Gyatso, Tenzin, His Holiness the Fourteenth Dalai Lama. *How to Practice: The Way to a Meaningful Life.* Translated and edited by Jeffrey Hopkins, PhD. New York: Atria Books, 2002.

Hahn, Thich Nhat. *Living Buddha, Living Christ.* New York: G. P. Putnam's Sons, 1995.

Hahn, Thich Nhat. *The Miracle of Mindfulness.* Translated by Mobi Ho. Boston: Beacon Press, 1976.

Hawking, Stephen. *A Brief History of Time.* New York: Bantam Books, 1996.

Hey, Tony and Patrick Walters. *The New Quantum Universe.* New York: Cambridge University Press, 2003.

Holy Bible, St. Joseph Edition. New York: Catholic Book Publishing Co., 1963.

Huxley, Aldous. *The Perennial Philosophy.* New York: Harper Collins, 2004.

Kaku, Michio. *Parallel Worlds.* New York: Doubleday, 2005.

Keating, Thomas. *Open Mind, Open Heart.* New York: Continuum, 1995.

Keller, Helen. *My Religion.* San Diego: The Book Tree, 2007.

Khema, Arya. *Being Nobody, Going Nowhere.* Boston: Wisdom Publications, 1987.

Koch, Christof. *Consciousness.* Cambridge: The MIT Press, 2012.

James, William. *The Varieties of Religious Experience.* New York: The Modern Library, 1994.

Kraus, Lawrence M. *The Fifth Essence, the Search for Dark Matter in the Universe.* New York: Basic Books, 1989.

Lee, Chwen Jiuan and Thomas Hand. *A Taste of Water.* Burlingame, CA: Fr. Thomas Hand, Mercy Center, 1990.

Merton, Thomas. *New Seeds of Contemplation.* New York: New Directions Pub. Corp., 2007.

O'Donohue, John. *Anam Cara: A Book of Celtic Wisdom.* New York: Cliff Street Books, 1997.

Randall, Lisa. *Warped Passages, Unravelling the Mysteries of the Universe's Hidden Dimensions.* New York: Harper Perennial, 2006.

Rinchen, Geshe Sonam. *The Three Principle Aspects of the Path*. Edited by Ruth Sonam. Ithaca, NY: Snow Lion, 1999.

Ruiz, Don Miguel. *The Four Agreements*. San Rafael, CA. Amber-Allen Publishing, 1997.

Smith, Huston. *The Illustrated World's Religions*. New York: Harper Collins, 1994.

Smith, Huston. *The World's Religions*. New York: Harper Collins, 1991.

Smolin, Lee. *Three Roads to Quantum Gravity*. New York: Basic Books, 2001.

Sogyal Rinpoche. *The Tibetan Book of Living and Dying*. Edited by Patrick Gaffney and Andrew Harvey. New York: Harper Collins, 1994.

Steinhard, Paul J. and Niel Turok. *The Endless Universe*. New York: Doubleday, 2007.

Teasdale, Wayne. *The Mystic Heart*. Novato, CA: New World Library, 2001.

Tolle, Eckhart. *A New Earth*. New York: Plume, 2005.

Tolle, Eckhart. *The Power of Now*. Novato, CA: New World Library, 1999.

Tsongkhapa, Lama. *The Great Treatise on the Stages of the Path to Enlightenment, Vols. 1-3*. Translated by The Lamrim Chenmo Translation Committee. Ithaca, NY: Snow Lion, 2000, 2002, 2004.

Tzu, Lao. *Tao Teh Ching*. Translated by John C. Wu. Boston: Shambala, 2006.

Tzu, Lao and Derek Lin. *Tao Teh Ching: Annotated and Explained*. Translated by John C. Wu. Woodstock, VT: Skylight Paths, 2006.

Wallace, B. Alan. *Hidden Dimensions, the Unification of Physics and Consciousness*. New York: Columbia University Press, 2007.

Webster's Seventh New Collegiate Dictionary. Springfield, MA: G. & C. Merriam Co., 1965.

Wolf, Fred Alan. *Time Loops and Space Twists*. San Antonio, TX: Hierophant Publishing, 2013.

Yeshe, Lama Thubten. *Introduction to Tantra, a Vision of Totality*. Edited by Jonathan Landaw. Boston: Wisdom Publications, 2002.

Yeshe, Lama Thubten and Jonathan Landaw. *Silent Mind, Holy Mind*. Ulverston, Cambria, England: Wisdom Culture, 1978.

Yeshe, Lama Thubten. *Universal Love*. Edited by Nicholas Ribush. Boston: Lama Yeshe Wisdom Archive, 2008.

Zopa, Lama Thubten. *Transforming Problems Into Happiness*. Edited by Ailsa Cameron and Robina Courtin. Boston: Wisdom Publications, 1993.